# Date Due

| | | | |
|---|---|---|---|
| for 4/15 | | | |
| 4/1. 5-30 | | | |
| 4/18 3:30 | | | |
| 4/20 3:45 | | | |
| 4/22 10:30 | | | |
| 4/24 3:15 | | | |
| 4-24 10:15 | | | |
| | | | |
| | | | |
| | | | |
| | | | |
| | | | |
| | | | |
| | | | |
| | | | |
| | | | |

# Traps to Avoid in Good Administration

Robert E. Bingham

**BROADMAN PRESS**
Nashville, Tennessee

© Copyright 1979 • Broadman Press.

4225-35
ISBN: 0-8054-2535

Dewey Decimal Classification: 254
Subject heading: CHURCH ADMINISTRATION

Library of Congress Catalog Card Number: 78-67265
Printed in the United States of America

Dedicated to the memory of

**Arthur B. Rutledge**

able administrator and Christian gentleman

# Foreword

My friend, Bob Bingham, is a dedicated, sensitive, caring, Christian gentleman. However, in this volume concerned with a basic and practical approach to management, he rips off our masks, exposes our sham efforts, and blasts away at our weaknesses. (He has them well-pegged). He then pulls the manager back together with practical counsel that is drawn from both excellent research and lived experiences.

Warning of the devious management traps that threaten all of us who, even in the most modest way, manage, Mr. Bingham skillfully indicates several options as to how these traps (management-killers) can be avoided. He is honest, straight talking, and, on occasion, extremely humorous in the presentation. However, through it all he cannot conceal the fact that he genuinely cares about us, his readers, and that his reward will be sincerely realized if we indeed become better managers. Or, if you prefer, stewards of the leadership trust that has been placed in our hands.

I place credibility in his counsel because I have seen him practice these principles at the Home Mission Board. Having served as administrator at two large, well-known churches, he also knows the traps laid out on the local church field.

WILLIAM G. TANNER

Executive Director-Treasurer
Home Mission Board, SBC

# Contents

# 1
# Strategy

*"Who's afraid of the big, bad wolf?"*

*Strategy is the planned use of all forces available to an administrator in order to achieve an objective.*

## A Case Study

Pastor John E. Smith was no loafer. His middle name should have been "Energetic." From his early college days he was a man-on-the-go. Excelling in academics, he was able to serve as a part-time pastor through his years of schooling. His early pastorates had been characterized by a zeal admired by his congregation. Having the drive and energy of two men, he could do many of the tasks usually left undone in the small churches.

Today Brother Smith is spending a week in the mountains taking stock of his ministry. Some might call it the *blues*. Others might term it a midcareer assessment or a vocational depression. One question seemed to surface and resurface: What went wrong?

John touched the obvious bases. (1) Family: above average physically and spiritually. (2) Spiritual barometer: steady, with some ups and downs. (3) Vocational calling: no doubt about it. God called him to serve his church and his people. (4) Attitude: healthy, with a steady desire to be the leader of the church (5) Economic barriers: negligible . . . and every expectation to continue to earn more than the cost of living increases each year. (6) Church acceptance: better than average. Receipts gently increasing, even though attendance is gently decreasing.

"Maybe it's just that time of the year," he thought. But that excuse did not account for the seriousness of his tireless question, "What went wrong?"

He began to review some specifics through the past five years. Maybe he could find reassurance in some of his better days. He jotted these incidents on a piece of paper.

1. Always attended the evangelism conferences.

2. Carefully wrote out a manuscript for every sermon.

3. Planned with the church council each first week in May.

4. If I want a thing done well, I always take the time to do it myself.

5. Decisions were made cautiously, usually based upon solid resources.

6. Seldom took a day off . . . just too much to get done.

7. While the church is not developing as it should, I guess we have not done too badly.

No question that John was working at being a good pastor. Yet it is obvious that he was falling into some of the most common traps known to administrators. He thinks these actions are positive assets on the ledger of his ministry. Not so. If he could only see the others (whose names are legion) who have knowingly followed in the same direction . . . only to find themselves entrapped. (Incidentally, all case studies used in this book are hypothetical except those relating to the author.)

## Strategy of this Book

This book is designed to help avoid such pitfalls as are common to Pastor Smith. Just a quick look at his checklist and a measurement against sound administrative principles will reveal the traps.

1. Good administration is done by achieving your objectives, not by engaging in activities. Conversions are objectives. Meetings are activities.

2. Effectiveness is more important than efficiency. A carefully prepared manuscript is efficiency, "doing the thing right." A sermon delivered effectively will bring congregational response, "doing the right thing."

3. Planning is a continuous process, not an event.

4. Delegation is a key tool for the successful administrator. It is poor stewardship of time for a $300-a-week-person to do the work of a volunteer.

5. Postwar strategy made decisions based primarily upon resources. For the future, good decisions will determine available resources.

6. Administrators measure time by results, not by hours.

7. Success for the disciple of Jesus is spelled p-e-r-f-e-c-t-i-o-n. It is not dependent upon how poorly someone else performs.

If you want to know more about these administrative principles, you will find them in the following chapters.

## Who's Afraid of the Big, Bad Wolf?

It is not unusual to see adults playing children's games. Fathers buy their young sons far-advanced electric model trains or sports equipment. Mothers revisit their childhood by helping their daughters make doll clothing. Maybe we are all only children growing up.

It is not newsworthy to discover adults playing children's games and failing to realize it. The Monday morning quarterback. The fire engine chaser. The CB radio operator. The Alice in Wonderland syndrome.

But it is tragic for adults to be playing childish games when the outcome has eternal consequences. It is humorous to play with your children and enact the role of the three little pigs crying, "Who's afraid of the big, bad wolf?" But it is disastrous to play "London Bridge is falling down," when in reality the Christian bridge to a needy world is falling down all about us—and maybe because of us.

Veteran ministers consistently acknowledge that their greatest need in effective leadership is to be skillful in the art of administration. It is paradoxical that the same group usually artfully dodges any early on attempt to acquire this skill through education and practice, principle and precept. They seem to equate sound administration and management with the "big, bad wolf." To the average vocational minister the very concept of administration has negative overtones. Could it be that we do not understand the field of management as it relates to the church and the denomination?

As in most ventures of life, church administration does not require continuous creativity. It is not a matter of knowing the most sophisticated principle of management. Most likely, it is avoiding some of the obvious mistakes of poor administration, especially when they seem to be logical, workable, and successful. But they only *seem* that way, for they actually are traps.

Everyone is going to make some administrative errors. But it may be disastrous when you think you are following sound management principles, only to find out that you have unknowingly fallen into a trap.

The purpose of this book is not to discuss administration in general; rather it is to isolate some classic traps that become lures to the churchman. A second glance at the table of contents will show the direction and location of the traps. If you must put the book down before a complete reading, at least you have been forewarned about them.

The word *traps* should be a warning. Traps indicate that someone or some force has been set against us with a purpose to fool us, detain us, or capture us. Maybe all three. Consider the fur trapper and his alluring cage with the temptables inside. Or the innumerable battlefield stories, where one force was fooled by the traps laid before by the opposition. Or the strategy of an athletic team when it traps the opposition into an awkward and indefensible position.

In each case the victim has been deliberately fooled into thinking that one course of action would be definitely advantageous, only to find out that it led to discontent, disillusionment, or defeat. And so it is with the Christian leader. The world, or Satan himself, has set many alluring traps. Few have the appearance of disaster. Some have the essence of innocence.

All are appealing on the outside. The effect of falling into any of the administration traps is emotionally expressed by the pop tune of the forties, "Laughing on the Outside, But Crying on the Inside." Take a second look at the case study. Pastor Smith may not have felt good enough to laugh about his condition. But as he enumerated the specifics, he probably was not aware that he had fallen into some deep traps. If you have not already done so, compare the two preceding lists. List 1 indicates the traps are tempting. List 2 states the administrative axioms that were perverted by the traps in list 1.

Football fans throughout the nation have picked up the chant of yelling "Defense . . . Defense." They have recognized one way to win the game is to prevent the opposition from scoring. In its essence, that is the strategy of avoiding the traps. Pushing the analogy further, when the offensive team allows the defensive guard to apparently get through unblocked, only to be blocked from the blind side, it is known as "trapping the guard." An effective guard seeks to avoid such an inviting trap.

No team ever won a game by preventing the opposition from scoring. And no administrator totally succeeds by avoiding traps. The best either could hope for is a tie. The offensive strategy of this book is designed to help you engage in action that will achieve your objectives and goals.

## So, Who Needs a Strategy?

As is so often the case, we are not even asking the right question. Every church leader has a strategy for accomplishing his objectives. Everyone knows we need a strategy. The real question is, How effective is our strategy? Since the environment has a great bearing upon any strategy for any occasion, this book will not deal with specifics. The outreach strategy for Old First Church, Big City, USA, would not be recognizable in King's Point Missionary Church, Dade County, Missouri. Similarly, the mission strategy overseas is not the same as in the United States.

Take your local situation. Superimpose your environment over your short- and long-range objectives. What is your strategy to accomplish your objectives? Consider yourself as the *coach* of your *team*. Your *players* have certain strengths and weaknesses. Your *opposition* has similar assets and liabilities. There are definable barriers in the way of achieving your objectives.

Your task as coach is to develop a plan to utilize all available resources in order to accomplish your objective. Perhaps you have seen a coach of an athletic team take over a losing team and transform it into a winner: same personnel, similar opposition, but different strategy.

As a leader of a part of the forces of the kingdom of God, have you stopped to consider the resources available to you? (Most of us are so busy overestimating the difficulty in reaching the objective that we tend to underestimate the available resources.) They, too, are legion and should be recognized by today's soldiers of the cross.

Herein lies a trap. When the opposition is so formidable and our forces seem impotent, we tend to flee like the Israelites from Pharaoh's army. Maybe we need to take a sheet from Joshua's notebook entitled, "A Strategy for Taking Jericho." But, carried to the extreme, that would be another trap. God seems to carry out his unusual acts only once. Only one strategy for Jericho. Only one burning bush. Only one Damascus Road. If Joshua, Moses, and Paul were living today, they probably would have tried to write a *Trilogy of God's Strategy:* (1) "Trumpets to Win a World"; (2) "Burn a Bush and Know God's Will"; (3) "Come to Damascus and Meet the Lord." Avoid the trap that God has a mimeographed strategy for his uniquely created soldiers and his complicated society.

A basic question is, What resources are available to you in your situation? What you do with them becomes your strategy. Some available resources are the physical environment, your personal gifts and talents, other human resources, and the collective financial resources. Yet, the Christian has more resources available than all the above put together and multiplied by the nth exponent. We have only to read the Word of God, the record of secular history, or recall our own pilgrimage to be reminded of the creative power and limitless resources of our God. Is it not academic to debate the availability of God's resources to those who are committed to his mission? The greatest trap to the Christian strategist is to overlook or underplay the importance of God's resources.

Our heritage and education may have given us a background that acknowledges all of the above as valid. Then why are we not achieving our personal and organizational goals? We may remind ourselves of the two beggars heatedly debating an academic issue. In a moment of frustration, one of the destitutes said, "If you are so smart, then why ain't you so rich?" Could the discrepancy between our ecclesiastical knowledge and our lack of achievement be that we are not administering those resources at our disposal? Could it be that we, like Moses, have tremendous resources available, but we have not picked up the rod of administration and used it in the name of Almighty God? If so, we have wandered in the wilderness, suffered spiritual and vocational famine, and stumbled into another trap—the trap of defying the value of good administration in the life of a religious organization, as well as in the life of a Christian leader.

## What Is Administration?

In order to practice successful administration, it seems appropriate to define it. But remember, being able to define *administration* does not guarantee that you will be an effective administrator. Some theoreticians would not recognize commonsense management if they met it on Main Street. It is neither "a big, bad wolf" nor "Mary's pet lamb!"

The American Management Association says *management* is getting things done *through* other people. The new manager emphasizes the phrase, "through other people." He is so enamored with his newfound responsibility that he wants to underline his authority. The veteran manager will empasize the phrase, "getting things done." He has learned that his goal is to get the job done.

Leslie E. This, author of *A Guide to Effective Management,* reflects a behavioral modification and says it is the art of developing people through work.

A basic definition for church administration might be achieving Christian objectives *with* other people. "The process of enabling the children of God, who comprise the body of Christ, the church, to become what, by God's grace, they can become, and to do what, by God's grace, they can do." [1] This may sound a bit weak from a position of strong leadership.

Why would we substitute the word *with* for the word *through?*
First, because sometimes it is difficult to tell who has the leadership position after a job has been well done. Secondly, our
Master warned us about always having to take the leading role.
He said that he who would be greatest among us must be
the servant of all. It seems that good administration is best
judged by the people who are not aware of any administration.
Maybe it is like government: he administers best who is least
observed to be administering.

Ministers, of all people, should seek to develop the attri-
bute of good administration. Just examine the word. Its root
form means relating to ministry. You have heard pastors say
that they were proclaimers, not administrators. The former
claim may or may not be true, according to the testimony of
the congregation and community. But you can be sure that
every minister is an administrator of some kind. The question
is whether we are effective or ineffective managers. If a pastor
is the latter, he had better find a person to help him who
can organize and administer. It is a strategy for survival.

Jillson and McLean say, "Management is at a watershed.
Our hope for the future rests on whether the manager as a
person can act from the best of his character and can work
toward implementing his highest values." [2] Others have simplified it to say that Christian principles must override any management principle. Yet, this is a source of a trap to say that a
management principle is contrary to a Christian principle.
Rather, it is a matter of one having priority and often being
complementary.

If you are looking for an example, examine the tactics of
Jesus who was not only the Master Teacher but also the Master
Strategist and Administrator. Did not he conceive of his entire
life as relating towards persons in regards to his Father's business? Recall his life as it involved planning, delegating, decision

making, motivating, evaluating, relating, and communicating.

*Planning*—Committing his work in the world to those twelve unlikely apostles has been called by many to be the boldest plan of man. Jesus was mindful of his plan when he reminded his followers that his time had not yet come.

*Delegating*—You can see this trait as Jesus sent out the seventy, made assignments to the apostles, and made provisions for the Last Supper. Even though he had all power and could make all things come to pass, he recognized the growth potential in his associates.

*Decision making*—He could make the difficult decisions. When it seemed apparent that he should be in Jerusalem, he went into Galilee. When his brothers warned him to avoid the center of the opposition's power structure, he "steadfastly set his face to go to Jerusalem" (Luke 9:51). He was willing to lose a battle in order to win the war. Jesus was truly a capital strategist.

*Motivating*—What wild claims Jesus laid upon his would-be disciples: "deny himself, and take up his cross, and follow me" (Matt. 16:24). But they did not completely do this until they were totally convinced that he was willing to give up his life for the cause that he espoused. After the resurrection they changed from lifeless cowards, running away from the garden of Gethsemane, to courageous leaders shaking their fists in the face of the same council that ordered the crucifixion of their leader. They were motivated unto their own death.

*Evaluating*—He could size up the potential and perform-ance of his followers *and* his opposition. His divine computer recall system helped him to see the value of Matthew, Nicode-mus, James and John, Andrew and Peter, and even the apostle Paul. Jesus evaluated his decision to set up his base of operations in his hometown after the people there rebelled at his teaching.

*Relating*—Has there ever been a person except Jesus who

could relate to all people with equal warmth? As we consider our station in life, could we effectively relate to persons like the woman at the well, King Herod, the rich young ruler, the demoniac, the Roman centurion, Mary and Martha, the lepers, the blind, the lame, the "ins and the outs," the "ups and the downs"? Perhaps the key is that he not only related to them as person to person but he also related them to his Father.

*Communicating*—Rabbis were known to be communicators. Jesus taught individuals, small groups, and multitudes in the thousands. He preached on the mountainside and the seashore. He was understood by the educated and the unlettered person. Cultured and barbarian, master and slave, rich and poor, rural and urban, thief and saint—all could understand his message if they chose.

Jesus' administrative posture can best be summed up with two quotations that show he had his objectives in mind from childhood through manhood. He organized his entire life around the spirit of, "Wist ye not that I must be about my Father's business?" (Luke 2:49). Also, "My meat is to do the will of him that sent me" (John 4:34).

## Your Management Style

Books, almost enough to fill the earth, have been written on mangement style. Some have viewed it from the behavioral sciences, and others took a corporate view. Some see the chief executive officer as a king of the domain, while others see him as an implementer of the personnel. We want to look at the style of a manager who is impelled to follow in the footsteps of Jesus.

Early on we must admit this is not easily done. Therein lies another trap: We pretend (or, at best, think) that our administrative actions are Christian. However, at times I have felt that I only ceremoniously "baptized" my actions with the use of a few carefully chosen words in the language of Zion. Before I knew it, I had fallen into the trap. That was embarrassing enough, but circling the rim of the trap were those whom I had tried to convince that my management style was based upon Christian principles.

As you consider your style, recall your last twelve months of leadership. Make your own appraisal of your style. Here are some criteria.

• Do I see my position as top sergeant or top servant? Do I serve the institution or does it serve me? Are my associates seen as people to do my bidding? Do I use my position to enhance my ego or my personal gain? Would I take the glory for a team job well done and blame the mistakes on my associates?

• Do the ends justify the means? Are my goals to be reached regardless of the consequences? Or, do I back off from my goals too easily, giving the excuse that they might offend someone? When I miss my target, do I pretend that I really was not trying. Or worse yet, do I shoot at the wall and then go draw the bull's-eye around wherever my shot hit the wall?

• Do I want my associates to call me by a respected title or by a personal name? Do I want to be known as a professional or as a person? Must people identify themselves to my secretary before I talk with them on the telephone? Is my "door always open," and just what does that mean? Do I return telephone calls as promptly as I want mine returned?

• How often do I say, "I made a mistake . . . You are right . . . We can do it together . . . Your help is really appreciated . . . What can I do to help with your task? . . . Give Joe the credit . . . I take full responsibility for the mistake . . . What is your opinion? . . . Do you think we are on course?"

• Am I timid about saying these words? There is a need to improve your performance. How are you using your time in relationship to our common goal? I would like to help you reach your potential. Our church's goal is more important than our petty whims and fancies. Our effectiveness is reduced by some of us hitting only on five cylinders.

• How do I want my associates to see me? Friend? Leader? Champ? Thinker? Foe? Doer? Shifty? Persuasive? Dictator? Successful? Egotistic? Spiritual? Laissez-faire? Humble? Aggressive? Gentle? Loser? Caring? Achiever? Cultural? Delegator? Clever? Buddy? Intellectual? Helper? Dynamic? Puppeteer? Father? Colaborer? Manager? Counselor? Manipulator? Second-miler? Professional? Organized? Decisive? Easy-to-know? Master?

• The basic question for the Christian administrator should be, How does Jesus see me? Review the above characteristics. Be as objective as possible in analyzing your management style as seen through the eyes of the Master. If you really want to know what your associates think of your style, give them an opportunity to anonymously evaluate your characteristics. (It must be completely anonymous, for only a fool would design a club with which his supervisor could beat him to death!)

## Why Develop a Management Strategy

What difference does it make? (Besides, a preacher is a minister, and not a manager.) Oh, oh, you just fell into the largest trap of all! Anyone who leads at least one other person to jointly accomplish a task is a manager. If you prefer the term *administrator,* use it. Call it what you will, today's Christian leader must take on the skills of blending the gifts and talents of the team's members into a combination that will achieve the group's goals.

Again we ask, What difference does a management strategy make? Actually, church or denominational agency examples are not easily recognized by all readers. Therefore, let us use two secular firms to prove the validity of sound management. As a boy in Kansas City I would often walk to the Montgomery Ward mail-order house to actually see my "wishes" on the retail floor. It was a giant organization. Last year I tried to return a gift that had been purchased at a Montgomery Ward outlet in a distant city. To my utter dismay, there is not a Ward's store in metropolitan Atlanta. What had happened in those forty years? Ward's had suffered a management crisis in the postwar years that is studied as a classic example by every marketing student. While top management was being hauled out of the penthouse office by United States marshals, Sears Roebuck was conducting management trainee programs for potential managers. Does it make a difference?

Look at a more recent example of Delta Air Lines. As a "new boy on the block," the struggling airline was having difficulty getting into the black figures that spell profit. They thought success depended upon experienced pilots. What did they care about good management? (Sound familiar?) After they set their management strategy in the early fifties, the company began to emerge as a top-level carrier. A case study may convince you that a management strategy may mean the difference between growth or death to your church or institution.

## A Case Study

In the mid-seventies the financial page of the *Atlanta Constitution* carried an arresting story. The quarterly statements of Delta and Eastern Air Lines were printed during the same week. Delta showed a ninety-million-dollar profit and Eastern was blushing under a ninety-million-dollar loss. An Eastern pilot confided that it was beyond his comprehension. They flew the same routes as Delta; used similar equipment; flew near-identical schedules. What could account for it? he asked. It was no secret to the business community. It was simply a case of superior management.

Shortly after this incident, Delta purchased Northeast Air Lines which operated mainly in New England. The former owners had operated in the red for the past sixteen quarters. Delta's management strategy took over using Northeast's former equipment, pilots, ground and office personnel. The management style was all that changed, with one exception, Delta showed a profit the first quarter of operation.

During the 1974 inflation/recession days, Delta was the only major airline which did not lay off any personnel. Management worked day and night to reassign work loads to assure that every employee had a job. Is it any wonder that when better times came to the country that every employee felt that Delta was *his* company!

Obviously, this was a genuine threat to Eastern. What could they do? They could have cried a lot. They could have doubled their advertising. They could have tried to hire Delta's pilots. No. They changed their management style, hiring Frank Borman. Mr. Borman, a public figure, was known as an astronaut. Eastern had plenty of capable pilots. The board of directors made Mr. Borman president because he was manager of ideas and people. An experienced air traveler will note the difference in the service of Eastern Air lines—just a different attitude about management.

## Spiritual Strategy

Could the religious community learn a lesson from this secular case study? Some churches and agencies are growing and expanding while others are contracting. "But you do not understand our situation." "We are in a depressed area." "Our people are moving out." "Yesterday's resources have dried up."

Watch out! There's another trap. It is so easy to make

excuses for our mistakes. We are so skillful in rationalizing that we can reason ourselves right out of existence. To be sure, many institutions have suffered, bled, and died in spite of heroic efforts to minister to the needs of the community. This is not a condemnation of them or their self-giving. However, many churches and agencies have suffered for the lack of management: upper, middle, and lower line of management. Some have been multistaffed organizations. Some have been served by one employee.

One might often wonder what would have happened if a sound administrative philosophy could have avoided some of these traps that must have ensnared them.

Let us suppose that your objective is to become an effective administrator in the task that God has called you to do. This would assume that, if you achieve your objective, you would feel fulfilled and God would be able to say, "Well done, thou good and faithful servant" (Matt. 25:21).

But wait a minute! Since you are reading a book such as this, you must want to become a better manager of the many resources at your disposal. You have considered the meaning and purpose of administration. You have looked as objectively as possible at your management style.

Now is the time to set your course in such a way as to become the type of administrator you want to be. That takes a determined strategy. The following chapters are designed to help you recognize and avoid some common traps in your pilgrimage. Perhaps you will recognize some of them. The key to increased effectiveness is understanding that traps usually appear as an enticement rather than a deterrent. (If the devil were really dressed in a red suit with a forked tail, no one would be tempted to follow him!)

In building your strategy, a critical trap is confusing an ally with the enemy. Ridiculous, you scoff. Be careful, that is the way to find yourself at the bottom of the trap. Unfortunately, many United States aircraft were shot down during the wars because they were falsely identified as the enemy.

If the church is engaged in mortal warfare with the forces of evil, it would behoove us to properly identify the friend or foe, the ally or the enemy! Some examples would be: thinking the enemy to be other Christian groups, constructive criticism, a disciplined approach to administration, Christian leaders who have a greater following than we, personal and corporate evaluation, peers who disagree with us, unusual methods of communication, honest doubt, other cultures, politics, power structures, and on and on.

When you stop to consider the great achievements of the great political and Christian heroes of the past, what do you recall? their physical characteristics? their education? their birthplace? their associates? their writings or speeches? When you think of Caesar, Alexander, Washington, Gladstone . . . or Kagawa, Carey, Wesley, Luther . . . or Peter, Andrew, James, John . . . do you not think primarily of their strategy to achieve their objectives? A great leader without a strategy is like a pilgrim without a map.

# 2
# Organization

*Organization is the arrangement whereby persons relate themselves to one another for accomplishing an objective*

## A Case Study

Pastor Jones is a gifted preacher, a man of vision, and well-prepared for his ministry in a metropolitan city. The church's search committee for the new pastor had found Pastor Jones's record in previous churches to be commendable. Although the former churches were smaller, the committee was confident he would adjust to the life-style of a larger and more complex congregation.

The first year was an extended honeymoon with the congregation. The Bride of Christ adored their new leader. Not only could he declare the Word of God in the place of worship but he also brought the Spirit of Christ into the homes of the congregation. Behold, a minister who could excel both as a pastor and a pulpiteer!

During the second year Pastor Jones continued to give of his energy to the needs of the church, collectively and individually. Someone suggested reviving the church council. The pastor did not object, but felt he could give his time in more personal ministries. The idea was lost for the want of a second. Yet the vital signs of a growing church were good and stable.

26

And the community liked the personable pastor.

Gradually, some disenchantment began to appear, slowly, subtly, but surely. It was hard to identify. It was most discernible in the questions asked by church leaders. "Do we expect to sell the property across the street?" "What are our plans for outreach in the community?" "Have you noticed the large turnover of our Sunday School staff?"

As members sought to discuss these growing tensions of church administration with the pastor, it was difficult to sit down and discuss the matter with him. Either he was preoccupied with other worthy matters, or he did not recognize the need of a better functioning church.

More serious questions soon surfaced. "Why isn't our church growing?" "Is our church being good stewards of our financial resources?" "Why are we having our revival the week before the Billy Graham Crusade?" "Why can't the deacons relieve the pastor of some visitation responsibilities?" "Why isn't my child getting better Bible study?"

The leadership began the inevitable arithmetic process of adding two and two to get four. What had happened to such a fine ministry? The positive ingredients remained positive. Why were there so many questions? Was there a missing ingredient in the recipe for successful leadership?

What do you think? Is administrative neglect common among church leaders? Is it your problem? Many a pastor has graduated from the seminary thinking he was not ready to be an administrator. Some persons zealously put down administrative responsibilities in the church.

As you read this chapter, look for possible helps for Pastor Jones (and you and me). What might help us avoid the trap of feeling that time spent in sound management methods is a waste of time?

## Locating the Traps

As you read the following questions, write your answer in the margin or underline your answer. At this point you may not be able to locate the trap. (Most traps are cleverly disguised, by design.) After you have completed the chapter, turn back to this page to see how well you were able to locate the traps.

- If you understand the principles of management, will that make you a good manager?
- Do you see yourself as a doer or an organizer?
- Do you see yourself as a thermostat or a thermometer?
- Would you rather be efficient or effective?
- Are you a problem solver or a problem preventer?
- Is it important for you to keep your hand on the pulse of everything?
- Do you see policies as personal or impersonal?
- Are management and leadership the same?
- Who manages the boss?

**Major Trap**—*Organization gets in my way. It keeps me from doing the things I need to do. It is all so structured and my ministry is based on a personal relationship.*

This is a tough trap to avoid. Very few of us were born with organizational skills. Most of us have some gifts or talents that enable us to be doers. It is much easier to continue to refine our skills as doers than to go through the discipline of being an organizer (manager or administrator).

We have seen some organizations that would drive a person to volunteer for the French Foreign Legion. They were the epitome of awkwardness. Cold, impersonal, and, to top it off, they were ineffective. So why have a millstone about your neck and call it "being organized"?

All of us have seen some creative, freewheeling spirits who

obviously were not organized. Some of them got lost on their way to work. Yet they seem to be successful. They are not encumbered with objectives, organizational charts, job descriptions, evaluations, and other unmentionables.

Looks appealing on the surface, doesn't it? That's what characterizes it as a trap. Anybody can recognize a hole in the ground; it takes discernment to recognize a trap. But stop and think a minute. Do the freewheelers usually run a one-man show? Does their ministry continue to grow as they continue to serve the local organization? Is this also true after they have left and gone on to greener pastures? Are they developing other leaders who will carry on? And, perhaps most important, did they accomplish the objectives they set out to achieve?

Beware of an adjoining trap which infers that understanding the principles of management will make a resourceful manager. This is no truer than knowing the multiplication tables will make an engineer. But avoiding the principles of arithmetic will prevent a person from becoming a successful engineer. Likewise, avoiding the principles of management will keep a person from becoming an effective administrator.

**Other Traps**—*1. I am a doer. I get things done. I lead churches by the sweat of my brow, long hours, and staying with the job. An organizer I am not. I have developed certain skills that I want to continue to use.*

We like to do things we have learned to do. They served us well when we had leadership of a small group and they will see us through this larger organization. (And into the trap we go!)

We continue to use old skills because we excel in demonstrating them. However, if a carpenter wants to break into the contracting business, he must sooner or later put aside his hammer and saw and pick up the telephone, slide rule, and adding machine.

An administrator is an organizer, not a skilled technician. Holding on to the latter will only jeopardize his growth as a manager.

*2. Every organization needs a problem-solver . . . somebody who has been there and knows how to get back. The trouble-shooter keeps the wheels rolling. My experience qualifies me as that person.*

Not so. It is better to prevent a problem than to solve one. Beware of the self-acclaimed problem-solver. Maybe he should know how to solve the problem; he probably created it in the first place.

Remember the old sermon illustration about the mountain curve that claimed so many casualities. The cars went too fast, overturned, and tumbled to the bottom. The local trouble-shooter established an emergency clinic at the bottom of the hill, and treated the continuing casualties. The problem preventer became distressed with this Band-Aid approach and put up warning signs, speed deterrents, and built a retaining wall around the curves QED.

*3. I must keep my finger on the pulse of the entire organization. The closer I am to the scene, the better I can respond to the needs. If I am going to be the manager of this outfit, I am going to manage all of it.*

The temptation here is not so much task-oriented as it is ego-centered. In other words, the ship can't sail unless I see to every task. I can do it better than anyone. I can't trust the other hands to follow through.

A logical symptom of the syndrome is for the boss to have almost everybody report directly to him. Or, he would second-guess and reorder any decisions made by one of his associates.

This pre-World War I management style can be seen today

in many large churches. It is rarely seen in the gigantic corporations who are respected in the financial world. They cannot afford such poor management at the top. It is a wonderment why some churches think they can afford such weighty belts around the waists of their lead runners. The race is too long and the competition too formidable.

*4. We don't need any written policies around our office. That's for large corporations. We exist like a family, and no family has written policies.*

This is one of the tougher traps to avoid because probably few people like written policies, except perhaps the person who writes them. Yet, Azarias reminded us that laws are not invented. They grow out of circumstance. As Thomas Paine said when he wrote in Revolutionary War times, "Society grows out of our virtues. Laws grow out of our vices."

It is true that few, if any, of us know families with written policies. But how many families do we know with one hundred children or five hundred or . . . ? Small groups have little need for multiple written policies. Usually they are verbally transmitted and mutually understood.

The time to have clearly established policies in any group is before the fact. Recall that God admonished Moses to use his writings to lead and teach the people. It's good preventive strategy.

*5. Everybody needs supervision, but who manages the boss?*

This is spoken as if every unit were autonomous. Even in hierarchial structures, the chief executive authority has supervision. In the corporate world, there is the board of directors to give counsel to the president. In the religious world, there is the local congregation, the synod, bishop, or the pope, depending upon your structure. Not to mention Almighty God, who continues to reign upon his throne.

This raises a primary question, Are not leaders and managers the same? What is the difference between the two? You can be a great leader without being a great manager. You cannot be a great manager without being a good leader. Joan of Arc was a great leader, but not a manager. Persons become leaders by definition when they have a following. Managers become managers when they accomplish objectives with others. Leaders become evident by the magnitude of the crowd that follows. Managers become evident by the magnitude of the objectives reached by the group.

Pastors, educators, missionaries, agency executives have an emotional hazard that makes it more appealing to lead than to manage. Call it an occupational hazard if you wish, but it is a syndrome that most of us inherit with our entrance into vocational ministry. Still not convinced? Which situation would the average leader favor? A large group of a hundred persons listening to the leader tell them something they probably already know, or a small group of ten persons planning how they expect to accomplish an agreed upon objective?

This is not to say that there is not a place for great leaders in our world, in our denominations, in our churches. It is to say there is a difference between leaders and managers. We need to assess our gifts and see where we can best exercise them in the kingdom enterprise.

## How to Avoid Organizational Traps

**General Guideline**—*Decide if you are a manager or a doer.* Basic to successfully tiptoeing through the traps is the answer to this question: Do you want to be a manager of people or a technician of skills? At first blush, everyone thinks he wants to climb the management ladder. That is, until he reaches a rung on which he is hung. Then he clamors for the good old days when he did not have so many decisions to make and so many problems to handle and so many people to supervise.

Remember the Peter Principle: "in a hierarchy, every employee tends to rise to his level of incompetence." [1] Many poor managers today were excellent technicians yesterday. Or, to put it another way: Some poor pastors of multi-staff churches were excellent pastors of a one-staff person church.

Use this little chart as a guide for personal appraisal. If you basically check No, forget the rest of this book. Resign any management responsibilities you have and pursue the skills that have stood so well by you in the past. However, if you seem to enjoy the management functions, then read on and avoid the organizational traps.

|  | Yes | No |
|---|---|---|
| A. I enjoy attending planning meetings. | ____ | ____ |
| B. I am willing to delegate projects in which I have experience and expertise. | ____ | ____ |
| C. I am willing to let an assistant perform a skill although I can do it more efficiently. | ____ | ____ |
| D. Budgeting is a challenge for me. | ____ | ____ |
| E. I see developing leadership as a vital part of my ministry. | ____ | ____ |
| F. I recognize that a certain amount of office work must be done at the expense of time spent in personal relations. | ____ | ____ |
| G. I can best be an agent of change through others. | ____ | ____ |
| H. Determining and maintaining policy is vital to my concept of administration. | ____ | ____ |

I. I feel the need of broad input from
associates in order to make decisions.    _____   _____

J. I am willing to struggle to make tough,
but important, decisions.    _____   _____

This in no way minimizes the doer. He is a most valuable person. Without doers, managers are needless. Both are necessary. We need doers in technical jobs and managers in administrative jobs. You may need the wisdom of Solomon to determine which traits you generally possess or to which pole you wish to be drawn.

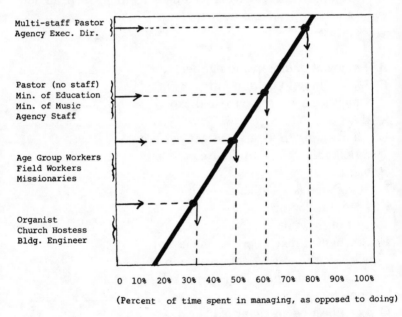

(Percent of time spent in managing, as opposed to doing)

The American Management Association makes good use of the principle seen in the above chart. Note the job titles on the left. Add whatever job you now hold, or might wish to hold, in your church or denomination. Basically they fall into three categories: upper, middle, or lower management.

The diagonal line indicates that everyone makes some administrative decisions and everyone makes some technical decisions. The placement of that line shows that managers are going to make more administrative decisions the higher they move up the management ladder. Likewise, the larger the administrative responsibility, the fewer technical decisions are his to make. In simple language, our total efforts can total only 100 percent. It is only a matter of how that percentage is divided.

A manager-oriented personality will be unhappy making only 30 percent of the administrative decisions. He will be restless and nonproductive. Similarly, the technically oriented person will go stir crazy if he cannot perform his skill. He wants others to be weighed down with decision making; just let him do his thing.

Dr. F. Townley Lord, past president of the Baptist World Alliance, gave me an excellent example of this principle when he was a member of First Baptist Church, Greenville, South Carolina. Pastor of Bloomsbury Central Baptist Church, London, England, for many years, he was amazed at the organizational abilities (and demands) upon the pastors in the United States. He marvelled at the concepts of Sunday School enlargement for all ages. Church administration was a totally new concept to him. Multimeetings per week of the congregation and committees took his breath. He continually praised the American minister as a master administrator. He confessed that it was foreign to him and to his English Baptist brothers of the pulpit.

You see, Dr. Lord was a preacher par excellence. Many acclaimed him to be the greatest preacher of the gospel they had ever heard. Another proof of his power to proclaim was the fact that preachers stood in line to hear him preach at evangelistic conferences. When he led the early morning devotional period at state conventions, which were usually poorly attended, the pews were packed before the morning session began.

It may be painful for us to hear Dr. Lord's assessment of the above situations. He said that American preachers were so involved in making the organizational machinery operate (managing) that they had little time to meditate, study, and prepare to preach (doing). To the contrary, Dr. Lord spent so much time in the technique of preaching that he had little time to manage. As a fact, he only went to the church building on Sundays and Wednesdays, except for weddings and funerals.

It was Dr. Lord's opinion that American pastors were superior administrators but average preachers. He saw some as trying to do both, and generally failing to achieve superiority in either. You may assess his opinion as tough or biased or totally inaccurate. Regardless, it puts flesh and blood on the otherwise cold and lifeless chart referred to above.

To avoid this basic organization trap, you must decide whether you wish to major on *managing* (achieving Christian objectives with other people) or on *doing* (performing a technical skill). Both are needed in the Christian leadership world. As you continue to read this book, you will find ways to avoid the traps that befall the manager.

**Specific Guidelines—***1. Understand the Organizational Approach to Management.* "Faith is the yeast of a good management system. You must trust in your people. Besides, it is more fun that way." This truism was spoken by the Sunday School director of Adult 5 Department, who also is now executive vice-president of the Woolworth Company. Lester Hewell understands organization, management, and people.

What application would Les make to a religious organization? Actually, this quotation was made in the context of the Sunday School task at Wieuca Road Church in Atlanta. Restated, it means that the manager must put complete faith in the organization as conceived by him and his people. Likewise, he must have faith in his people to carry out the objectives of the organization just as faithfully as he wants to achieve these objectives.

Few church leaders are as effective as they want to be. This is probably because they see themselves as a one-man gang marching off in all directions to subdue the forces of evil. As a result, too many church leaders do not manage their jobs— their jobs manage them.

The underlying premise of a fruitful organization is that good administration allows the manager to extend his ideas and influence through others in order to multiply his labors. One of the rewards of a minister of education is to walk throughout the educational facilities on Monday and see the evidence of his teaching on the chalkboards, corkboards, interest centers, and the like. I always felt the most productive part of my week was the teachers' improvement period on Wednesday and Sunday nights. About eight hours a week were invested in preparing for these two training periods. The adult teachers were faithful in attendance and interest.

In effect, I was a teacher of teachers. Although I did not regularly teach an adult Bible class, I was able to extend my ideas to about seven hundred adults every Sunday.

There is an unnoticed advantage to a religious organization. It is one that many modern corporations are only beginning to recognize. This "light hidden under a basket" came to my attention at several national seminars I attended in the general field of management. Only a few religious administrators were present, and we were outnumbered by vice-presidents of well-known, national corporations.

After the second day of interparticipant dialogue, the religious conferees began to be approached at lunch or during coffee break time. The corporate executives were wanting to draw on our experience. How odd! How unexpected! We went to the seminar for exactly the opposite reason, to draw upon the experience of these professional managers. What could possibly account for the switch?

In an unofficial clergy caucus, we sought answers to the switch. Finally, we made sense of the situation. Corporations had dealt with employees for years under the assumption that you could inspire loyal service through the incentive of salary compensation. In the last two decades, management has found out that job fulfillment is the primary motivator among employees. Financial compensation is usually fourth or fifth from the top.

Religious leaders have operated under that premise for two thousand years. Now, church administrators have become the sought-after and have become the experienced persons in the field of motivation. An important corollary should be noted. The use of volunteers has been discovered only recently by the business community. Who has had more experience in utilizing volunteer help than the church? What we need to do is to capitalize upon our organizational uniqueness.

2. *State the Purpose and Objectives of Your Organization.* The famous last words of many a trap-fallen person are, "Who needs to state his purpose? If a person doesn't know his purpose, he deserves to fall into a trap. Ooooooops!"

If you cannot reduce your purpose and objectives into writing, they probably are not clear to you. Certainly they are not clear to others in your organization.

Your *purpose* should be the overall reason for the existence of your organization. It should be so challenging that it is impossible to attain. Your *objectives* should be so carefully stated that if you attain them, you will come as close as possible to achieving your purpose. Objectives are timeless and undated because they relate to your timeless challenge.

Your *goals* are measurable and dated. They are bits of your objective. Just as you cannot chew and digest a whole meal with one bite, you cannot achieve a worthy objective with one goal. Several well-conceived and reachable goals can greatly assist you in attaining your objective.

If you are looking for definitions, here are some generally accepted ones.

Purpose—the basic reason(s) for which a program exists

Objective—specified ends established for an indefinite length of time through which the general purpose of a program can be achieved and which may be translated into goals and actions

Goal—a statement of dated intent to obtain a measurable quality and/or quantity of results in keeping with an objective

Study this diagram and its explanation to see if it is not a logical way to achieve the results you wish from your organization.

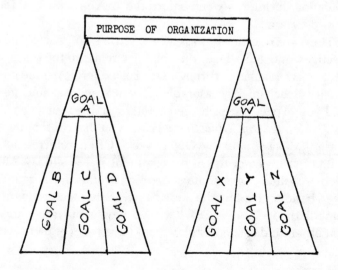

Using the church as our model, let us suppose that the purpose of a local congregation is to share the gospel of Jesus throughout the world. You may wish to restate and refine it, but that is a worthy purpose and obviously unattainable for a local congregation. But the church can continue to be faithful in identifying with that universal purpose.

Perhaps two of the objectives that directly relate to the purpose might be: to give every person in our community an opportunity to hear the gospel within the next five years and to give every person in our community an opportunity to belong to a New Testament fellowship.

As a wise manager, you would then divide the scope of each objective into several goals. The goals for the first objective might include: increase baptisms by 30 percent during the next year; increase Bible study attendance by 30 percent during the next year; sponsor a local evangelistic television program during prime time during the week before Easter; enlist other Christian churches in the community in a "Witness Blitz," attempting to witness personally to 20 percent of the population during the week before the above-mentioned television program.

Here are questions to ask when setting up your purpose, objectives, and goals. Does the objective relate to the purpose? Is the object reachable through sacrificial effort? Are the goals specific? Reachable? Measurable? If you reach the four goals could you expect to reach the objective in five years?

3. *Manage by Objectives.* Have you heard the magic phrase, "Management by Objectives?" Often referred to as "M.B.O." It is one of the in management systems today. Most effective systems have some spin-off of Professor George Odiorne's basic concept by the same name.[2] Other leaders in management theory may ask, What is so new about the phrase? What other kind of successful systems have we ever had except

ones that manage through the reaching of objectives? Odiorne has only spotlighted the fact for us and precipitated a flood of specific management systems directly related to his stated principles.

Then why all the fuss about the need to manage by objectives? You are now standing at the edge of a great trap and seeing multitudes of administrators who thought they were managing by objectives. Alas, in fact, they were managing by activities. They may have actually reached all the designed activities, which they erroneously thought were goals. But in doing so, they did not achieve their objective, more easily understood as "results."

Using our above model, here are some intended goals that are not bonafide goals. They are activities. They may or may not actually achieve the results needed to assist in reaching the organization's objective which is, To give every person in our community an opportunity to hear the gospel in the next five years. Goal A—Conduct witness training courses twice each year. Goal B—Organize neighborhood prayer groups throughout the city. Goal C—Lead a study in the book of Acts on Wednesday nights. Goal D—Preach evangelistic sermons regularly.

Now ask yourself the magic question: If the church actually achieved each goal, could they expect to reach their objective in five years? Probably not. These "goals" are activities. They may or may not result in objective achievement.

There is such a fine line between activities and goals, and the trap is very tempting. Let us further differentiate between the two. The first goals, if reached, will result specifically in a measurable number of persons in the community hearing the gospel. In the second set, activities have been set in motion that may support such evangelistic goals, but do not guarantee objective achievement. The sad conclusion of the trap is that the manager thinks he is going to succeed because he actually does lead the congregation to perform admirably each of the so-called goals.

After five years the manager is surprised to learn that everyone in the community has not heard the gospel. And why not? The church had fulfilled each goal each year. Too late he discovers that he had no real goals at all. Most churches plan and arrange by activities, and regretfully, do not achieve their intended objectives.

*4. Understand the Functions of the Organization.* Every successful organization performs these five functions (by one name or another): plan, organize, motivate, coordinate, control. Oversimplified, the managers devise plans they believe will accomplish the given objectives. They organize their human, physical, and financial resources with the expectation of reaching goals that will accomplish the objectives. They motivate all personnel to adopt the objectives and goals as "ours" rather than "theirs." They provide effective coordination of all factors involved in the collective achievement of the objectives. And finally, the managers make sure there are adequate controls provided to ensure that the organization will reach the stated objectives if every person involved performs reasonably well.

Note that every function relates directly to the stated objectives. Therein is the unity of the organization. Every person is contributing a segment of the whole. "The whole is equal to the sum of the parts." That might be a geometric axiom. But in Christian "geometry" we have the advantage of "the whole exceeding the sum of the parts." You readily recognize this is due to the presence of the Holy Spirit. Physical scientists call it synergism. Christians call it spiritual power!

President of General Motors, the pope of the Roman Catholic Church, the pastor of a local church, the chairman of a finance committee, and the executive of an agency—all have one thing in common. They all must plan, organize, motivate, coordinate, and control. The only difference is the magnitude and intensity of their function.

*Caution sign!* Do not adopt any management system until you have weighed the pluses and minuses of how it will improve the human-relation factors in your organization. Adolf Hitler had an efficient organization, but the negative human relation factors had as much to do with his defeat as any other factor. Take care in designing your organization. It can be very dynamic for good or for evil.

## A Case Study

Pastor Jackson has had five years at First Church and generally they could be summed up as happy years. His family was happy and settled. The congregation was happy and satisfied. Pastor Jackson was happy on the outside, but frustrated on the inside. Why did the powerful army of the church seem to perform like dwarfs wearing boots, sloughing their way against the devastating forces of evil? He felt like he was fighting the battle of good and evil all by himself. What could be done? Surely something more was needed than another committee meeting.

The church council was timid when first consulted. They were happy with their pastor. Why rock the boat? Did he really want their opinion or merely confirmation of his? Finally a local merchant commented that he felt the church was far more important and complex than his business. The pastor pressed for a reason for the lack of organization in the church. The council admitted that every organization of the church seemed independent of the others. They lacked a common goal and directed leadership.

The pastor was taken aback by their frankness but could not deny their wisdom. Five years had built a trust relationship which allowed him to ask what could be done to increase the effectiveness of the many church programs?

From this felt need the council, under the pastor's guidance, began to study the Scriptures and other books on the function of a church and how to organize the resources of the congregation to meet the challenge.

Soon a five-year plan emerged and was adopted by the church. Goals were set and individuals and groups were assigned responsibilities. The council agreed to serve as the coordinating group for the many tasks assigned. Each task was vital to accomplishing the agreed-upon goals.

All organizations of the church felt important because they had specific tasks to achieve. For the first time they felt a part of the whole (the church), which was far more important than their segment (their organization). The pastor now is not the only executive officer of the church. He is the chief executive officer. In this role he is in control of the body of Christ with its many and diverse parts. Now he feels that all parts and all people are truly administrating the function of the church.

What would be your prediction for Pastor Jackson and people for the ensuing five years? They have avoided one of the most debilitating traps, equating organization as an unnecessary evil.

# 3
# Planning

**"Any fool can draft a five-year plan."**

*Planning is the determination of what needs to be done, who needs to do it, by what time, in order to accomplish an objective.*

## A Case Study

Jack Baker was serving as a foreign missionary, specializing in communications. While the stated objective of this mission was evangelistic in nature, no evangelist alive could surpass Jack's concern and interest in communicating the gospel. Although not a preacher, Jack was the needed link in transmitting the Word into words that flowed over the airways.

His technical training disciplined him to accept no excuse for perfection in the technical aspects of clear communication and reception. Electronics was his expertise, yet he was a man of personal devotion and spiritual commitment. He was just the man God needed in God's plan of world missions.

The leader of the mission was J. T. Adams, a field evangelist with thirty years experience in the area. He was both knowledgeable and persuasive in understanding the culture of the people and articulating the gospel in their language. He was a master in mass preaching, as well as personal witnessing. The other missionaries looked up to him spiritually and professionally.

It was time for the annual mission conference, one year after Jack had arrived on the scene. Everything seemed to

45

be just right—good fellowship, excellent Bible study and times of devotion, stirring preaching, wholesome evaluation of the past, and vision for the future.

On the third day of the meetings, a natural conflict of objectives arose. In making their plans for the future, there were some concepts that did not lend themselves to effective planning. Oversimplified, they were: (1) Each missionary felt his input was equal to every other missionary in every field of endeavor. (2) The chairman served as moderator, but was not an action-maker. (3) Everyone tended to support every idea submitted, rather than to offend the initiator of the idea. (4) Plans seemed to be too general and were related to personal whims rather than specific goals of the mission as a whole. (5) In order to get some consensus, the missionaries began to trade-off one idea for another. (6) There was a deep feeling of personal warmth and care, but no feeling of mission cohesiveness. (7) Everybody was doing what was right in their own eyes, but no one had collective vision. (8) There was a growing concept that if they each chipped away at their own rocks, one day they would have a great sculptured mission work for the Lord.

Chairman Adams sensed the frustration and took the meeting into his own hands. He challenged everyone present by saying, "All of us are committed Christians, on a mission for our Lord. Everyone is important and needed. Each has a specific task to accomplish. But we are not united in our objective. It seems that we are mounting our horses and riding off in all directions. We have agreed that our primary objective these five years is to give every person in our country an opportunity to hear the gospel. All agreed? Of course. But we fail to see that our combined efforts as a whole will total more than our individual efforts.

"Jack, you are invaluable as our communication expert

and technician, but are you giving your total energies to accomplishing our mission's objective? It seems that your objective is to produce a perfect electronic signal. Maybe the time you spend trying to move from 95 percent efficiency to 100 percent could be spent in personal witnessing through some home Bible study classes."

The lid was off the can and out came the worms. Jack reacted by pointing out there was an element of truth in Adam's comments. But he reminded the group that they were still trying to evangelize the country with the same basic communication philosophy as they did thirty years ago, Telstar not withstanding.

Sally, the home-and-church-mother, rationalized that being a good mother and wife was enough. When she added being the schoolteacher for their children, that was surely worthy of the objective of the mission.

Bud, the agricultural missionary, confessed that his goal was assisting the farmers to meet the physical needs of the locality by providing more irrigation for more food. Yes, he tried to set a good Christian example in word and deed. But his priority as a missionary lay in agriculture, not evangelism. That was Adam's job.

The seminary professors were caught up in academics. They were giving time-and-a-half in their teaching roles. But they were not seeing the overarching objective of the mission as dictating priorities for their tasks.

Finally a voice came from the rear of the room, "Why don't we follow our plan? Remember three years ago when we all put the pieces of our work in place? Our puzzle of frustration became a challenging mosaic? Why not use our plan?"

With one accord the group seemed to respond, "What plan?"

## Locating the Traps

- Thinking that planning is unimportant.
- Thinking that planning is everything.
- Everyone plans every day—it's simple.
- It's too complex for the nonprofessional.
- Whatever my boss plans will suit me.
- Just get a good slogan and stick with it.
- Planning is an annual event with us.
- It is only sophisticated gimmickry.
- It's not biblical or theological.

**Major Trap**—*Any fool can draft a five-year plan. It takes a creative leader to be able to make day-to-day adjustments as the crises arise. The times change so fast that yesterday's planning is obsolete, tomorrow's planning is dreaming.*

This is the first great watershed in management. To plan or not to plan, that is the question. To be sure there have been classic cases of extremism on both sides of the question. Some churches seem to plan the morning worship service between hymns. Others make plans for year A.D. 2000 that are set in concrete today. Either extreme is doomed to die. It just takes a few years longer for the latter to be pronounced dead.

An illustration in management training is the person running up to the railroad ticket window and pleading, "I've got to go five hundred miles. Give me a ticket before the train pulls out. Don't bother me about a specific destination. Can't you see the train is about to leave? No, I don't want to know what time it gets here. I just don't want to be late leaving."

Modern transportation has not changed the aptness of the analogy. It has only changed the acceleration by which the consequences are more dramatic. After all, you could get off the train at the next station when you found you were really going in the wrong direction. Some people were known to jump from the train before it got up a full head of steam. Today's life-style makes planning, changing at the last minute, about as risky as jumping out of the airplane on takeoff.

Several questions should serve as caution lights to those about to fall into the trap of feeling that planning is not essenial to good administration.

1) If you do not know your destination, how can you decide how to get there?

2) If you do not know where you are going, how will you know when you arrive?

3) If you are going at a great speed, is it in the right direction?

**Other Traps**—*1. Long-range planning is a calculated way to make sure you cannot see the trees or the forest. You overlook the immediate needs of the organization by planning far in advance. And no one can predict what will happen in ten, or twenty years. You neither get to eat your cake nor keep it. Planning one year in advance is a strain on anyone's prophetic ability.*

These might well have been the famous last words of Rommel in Africa, or Napoleon and Hitler in Russia. It was fortunate for democracy that these generals had such errant planning models. It may be just as tragic for the kingdom that so many Christian leaders, missionaries, pastors, laypersons, have just as errant concepts of planning.

*2. Whatever my boss wants to plan will suit me just fine. He's the leader and calls all the shots. I just try to follow through and do my part.*

Spoken like a loyal soldier of the cross. And like a person who is destined for stagnation of creativity. It is one thing to be loyal to your leadership. It is a different thing to assume that you can blindly follow any plan that is effected and still accomplish your personal goals.

If your goals (both structural and personal) are in conflict with those of your organization, you have three basic alternatives. (1) Try to amend the organization's goals. (2) Try to change your goals. (3) Find another organization that has compatible goals with yours.

For the Christian, a more basic question arises: Are my goals and the goals of my organization compatible with the purpose of the kingdom? Common strategy dictates that Christians need to find out what God is doing and planning and get on with it.

An illustration used in *Serving with the Saints* [1] is an appropriate analogy. A staff member in a Christian organization may not be *the* leader, but he may be the leader of his unit. By his education, experience, and expertise he may be the best prepared to lead in a certain task. But he takes his general leadership from the leader of the entire organization. The leader of the trombone section takes his structural guidance from the concertmaster of the orchestra. Yet, both of them cue-in from the conductor. In the church, the minister of music is the leader of that segment of the church's ministry. However, he takes his cue from the general leadership of the pastor. But both of them accept the planning and direction from Christ, the Master of the entire organization.

*3. Just get a good slogan and plan around it. Everyone knows that major business companies have used this technique for years. Remember what it did for Alka-Seltzer? "Try it: you'll like it!" "I can't believe I ate the whole thing." Biblical comics even claimed those were the original words of Adam and Eve in the garden.*

Schaller and Tidwell refer to this as planning by clichés. [2] "All too often simplistic clichés, which later turn out to be fallacies, are offered as the solution to the problems of the church." For example, ours is a friendly church, and that's our main attraction for people. Others are: (1) The youth are the church of tomorrow. (2) If we are ever going to reach more people, we will have to move to another location. (3) If we can bring in programs to our church building during the week, we will fill our sanctuary on Sunday and our membership will increase.

A tricky-play-on-words-slogan can no more provide a basis for planning, than the slogan "Everyone Win One" can guarantee a successful evangelistic program. At best, a slogan can only capture the imagination of your public and capsulize your goal into a memorable phrase.

*4. Planning is an annual event in our organization. We all take time off for a week and give our best thoughts toward our plans for the coming year. We develop objectives, goals, and actions and type it up into a neat booklet for everyone to have on his desk.* Sounds good. It is not bad. It just prevents us from doing our best, and that may be the most insidious trap of all.

Planning is a process, not an event. It must go on continually, or it is destined for an early demise. The last factor in the process is evaluation and redesign, and the cycle begins again. The above illustration probably ends up with the booklet filed away in obscurity or ostentatiously placed on the desk for display purposes. A real plan book is dog-eared and penciled throughout. It is like a needed road map through unfamiliar territory. It is kept close by for ready reference.

*5. Everyone must plan to exist. What's the big deal about that? Tell me something new. We plan every staff meeting. You fellows try to make something complicated out of something as inherent as breathing.* Sounds impressive. Maybe he is a natural planner, maybe not. More than likely his staff associates have a different response to his planning style. They might say, "We don't do any planning. It sounds simple enough to him when he says, 'Look here! Our purpose is to have more Christians and better disciples in our organization. Now, let's get out there and get the job done.' " If the example were not so true, it would be humorous rather than tragic.

*6. Planning is only window dressing, substantiated by pages of statistics—more properly called "statics." If we see enough pages of figures, charts, and graphs, we believe most anything.*

It is true that statistics turn off many people. They either cannot understand them or cannot believe them. Which one of us has not quoted one of these accusations: "Figures don't lie, but liars figure"; "He who lives by statistics will die by statistics."

Planning may be used by some groups for window dressing, but it is the lifeline of any organization that has succeeded in accomplishing its objective. The plan need not be sophisticated, but you can rely on the fact there was a plan: well-conceived, well-understood, well-implemented, and well-evaluated.

*7. Only trained professionals can really plan. Ask one of them to come in and help us. You don't expect a plumber to practice law nor the attorney to lay the pipes for a new home. Get a pro to do it for us.*

Like most traps, these are half-truths to misguide us. Professional consultants can give guidance and insight to organizations as they begin their planning process. But the leadership of the organization are most likely to put all the pieces together for an effective plan. You know your environment, your human and financial resources, and the barriers toward accomplishing your objective. You know the gifts and talents of your personnel to match the needs of the tasks to be done.

But another word of caution—you may be too close to the trees to see the forest or too blind to see the trees. Remember Amos, the unlikely moonlighter from Judah. He was not the outside professional nor the inside experienced practitioner. He was God's man to serve as the consultant to Israel. Avoiding this trap might mean that we must look to God for direction in our planning using whomever and whatever he chooses to use in the process.

## Questionnaire

If you can truthfully answer yes to each of the following questions, turn immediately to chapter 4. If not, the balance of this chapter will help you to get the feel of the basics in improving your planning procedures.

Yes   No

1. Planning is a continuing process.
2. My objectives are clearly stated.
3. My goals are realistic and measurable.
4. Planning takes at least 10 percent of my time.
5. My long-range plans have current implementation.
6. My personal objectives are compatible with the objectives of my organization.
7. I plan from a basis of strength not weakness.
8. My plans set direction. I expect to make exceptions.
9. I have implemented this year's plans this month.
10. A shallow planner seldom makes a deep impression.
11. I know the vital steps in the planning process.

_____  _____  12. I know the basis of program planning to budget planning.
_____  _____  13. Deadlines are a built-in security system.
_____  _____  14. Always evaluate the last year's results before finalizing next year's plans.
_____  _____  15. Past failures are a vital ingredient to future planning.

## How to Avoid the Planning Traps

**General Guidelines**—*1. Jesus practiced and taught good planning.* Look at his entire life as recorded in the Gospels. He was a master in knowing exactly where he was in his time line related to his purpose and objectives. He advised his family that they did not understand his plan. He took about two decades to do his planning and only three years to carry out these plans.

Recall Jesus' teaching in Luke 14:28–30 when he warned that if a man wanted to build a tower, he had better stop to count the cost to see if he could complete it. Otherwise, if he was unable to finish it he would subject himself to ridicule. Today, Jesus might have included bankruptcy!

Some people claim that planning short-circuits the work of the Holy Spirit. How could the teachings of Jesus be in conflict with the work of his Spirit? Planning need not preempt the Spirit, but it can enable the Spirit to do his work more effectively. People who excuse themselves from planning based on the above theology may be more lazy than orthodox.

*2. It may have helped Jesus, but how can it help me?* A good plan should be the basis of your program, your decisions, and your control. It helps you get something accomplished, instead of just wishing you could get it done.

*3. Recognize that planning is essential to living.* The person who says, I don't believe in planning does not realize what he is saying. Human existence is dependent upon individual and collective planning, conscious or subconscious. When you get up in the morning, you choose what clothing to wear based upon your anticipated activities that day. You pay your bills at the end of the month in terms of your plans for credit, savings, and future purchases. Your financial security is dependent upon your plans for retirement, the government's plans for Social Security, and your savings investment plans. Or, you have a plan that says all of these are not helpful to you in reaching your objective, and your plan is to take each day as it comes. Unfortunately, that plan usually takes into consideration that if you fail, some other persons or institutions will bail you out!

Almost everyone plans. Some plans are good, some poor; some near-sighted, some farsighted; some selfish, some unselfish; some relate to objectives, some do not. Almost everyone plans. But almost everyone walks, too. Some walk at the infant's pace, and some walk at Olympic pace.

Likewise, there is a quality to planning, and it is just as dramatic as the difference in the toddler and the gold medal winner. A shallow planner seldom makes a deep impression. Many leaders are impressive at first glance. They can move masses of people to make quick decisions. They can gain a following based upon the here and now. However, without balanced planning, their leadership remains static and their adherents dwindle.

4. *Long-range plans must include the quality of vision but not be visionary.* The latter quality tends to be without reason and credibility. The former requires an element of faith in order to achieve the objective. Long-range planning is seldom effective beyond five to ten years. But vision can span a

decade or two. How can you have a long-range plan and begin each year with a shock to the organizational system called, "Surprise!?"

Daily implementation, if not in action at least in mind-set, is necessary for two reasons. First, if your plans for the next five years cannot be acted on today, the plans are not valuable today. And today is the only day you have. If they only have a future sense about them, the realism absent today will most likely be unrealistic in the future. Searching through the twenty-four cases of files of Mrs. Una Roberts Lawrence, noted writer, editor, and historian for Southern Baptists in the first half of this century, I found that she had predicted that women would begin to assume more leadership in our churches by the year 1975. Her files showed that she worked at that cause from 1910 until her death in 1973.

5. *Planning affects more than dollars and budgets, far more.* Actually, dollars only supply the financial basis for our objectives. They are not, or should not be, our objectives. Religious institutions are not in the business of accumulating and saving money. We are involved in investing our faith in the lives of others. In that process we may have to erect buildings, finance salaries, and support programs of work. Therefore, plans for our organizations involve spending money through wise planning.

6. *Planning is a tool.* It does not take the place of administration or promotion. The Inter-Agency Council of the Southern Baptist Convention adopted its plan for planning in 1978. The following material came from their research.

Like any other tool, it may be wrongly used, as when it is substituted for action and decision, or when it becomes an evasion from the difficult tasks of management. It may also be wrongly used when it is developed without adequate understanding and applied without thorough follow-through.

Planning is merely the application of common sense to future work. It is not a predetermination of the future. Rather, it is an intelligent estimate of what the future will be like, and a procedure for dealing with it in an efficient manner. Planning is the projection of the realization or achievement of a program. Its chief value is that it helps us to know what decisions to make now, and what is possible in the future.

7. *Usable plans come off of objectives.* What are some qualities of good objectives? Oversimplified, they are:

1. Related to your purpose
2. Limited in number
3. Attainable
4. Challenging
5. Measurable
6. Specific
7. Related to plans of other units in your organization

**Specific Guidelines—***1. The chief executive officer of your organization must believe in and practice planning or forget it structurally.* You can plan personally, but do not waste your time in organizational planning without the example and support of your leader.

*2. Understand the steps in a sound planning process.* The diagram on page 58 shows the process of the Home Mission Board of the Southern Baptist Convention. The organization determines the following:

1. Statement of purpose
2. Environment (situation in which you do your work)
3. Objectives
4. Goals
5. Action plan
6. Evaluation

*3. Base your budget on your tasks in your action plan priorities.* So often churches get these two reversed. Often,

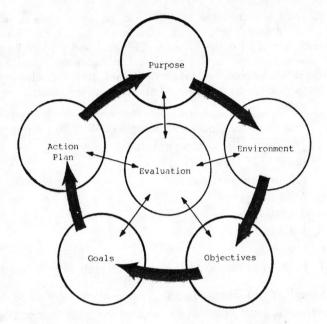

the finance committee decides on what the total amount of the budget should be. Then the church council plans next year's program off of that base. A budget is only a road map allowing your church to reach her objectives through programs of work.

*4. Plan with people and priorities in mind.* Granted that your organization may take on new persons in the future, your plans begin with those now in your organization. What are their skills, gifts, and talents? How do they fit into the achieving of your objectives? Survey the tasks to be done and strive to match up your people with the tasks. Get the round pegs in the round holes.

The word *people* sounds so warm. *Priorities* sounds so cold. At its coldest, priorities keep people from doing what they want to do when that is contrary to the objective of the group. The apostles had one set of objectives. Jesus had another. The apostles were often frustrated when Jesus determined to follow his priority system rather than theirs. That's the price of leadership. It goes with the territory.

5. *Develop a calendar with deadline dates and specific assignments.* An insurance executive put it bluntly when he said that in his company people are not motivated as much by what you "expect," as by what you "inspect." It did not sound right. It did not square with my concept of Christian leadership. Since our deacons' family ministry plan was only operating at 35 percent efficiency, his concept was worth the risk.

The following year *we* did note our common objective: to visit every family of the church during the year, and at crisis times as needed. One small addition was made to the plan. We agreed that each month a sheet would be printed and distributed at the deacons' meeting. Each deacon's name, number of families, number of families visited to date, was listed on the sheet. Are you surprised that our efficiency leaped to 94 percent that year?

Deadlines are a friend to the achiever. They are an abomination to the dreamer. They help us reach our intended goal if we take them one at a time. Merrill Moore used to proclaim, "Life is hard by the yard; by the inch, it is a cinch."

6. *Many a well-meaning rookie has gone through the whole planning cycle except evaluation.* The process helped, so it was concluded to do it again next year. And the next year. And so on. And that is why some horse and buggy companies folded when the automobile was invented. They did not reevaluate their purpose and objectives. No one misses the carriages. Tragically, many churches have failed for the same reason, and we miss them. Don't let yours be the next to be missed because you failed to evaluate your plan each year, correcting and improving as you go.

R. O. Loen, president of a management consulting firm, gives this advice, "Get the facts before they get you." [3] He then goes on to say that the following questions are basic in evaluating.

1. What deviations from planned performance are significant?
2. What caused such deviations?
3. What actions might you take?
4. What are likely results of each action?

7. *Be aware of the traps to effective planning.* Leslie This interviewed one hundred managers and accumulated this list in descending rank order.[4]

1. Inadequate communication
2. Insufficient data
3. Faulty or inadequate problem identification or definition
4. Insufficient time to plan
5. Unclear parameters for the plan (staff, budget, time, facilities, equipment, etc.) in the planning request
6. No emphasis on planning; the organization prefers to work on a crisis basis
7. I don't like to plan.
8. Nobody will cooperate in the planning process.
9. We don't have a range of alternatives to choose from in our planning.
10. The timing is bad for submitting plans.
11. The knowledge or views of the planners are too limited.
12. My organization resists change.
13. We don't know the organization's major goals; objectives are not clear.
14. We don't involve the people who have to implement the plan or who are affected by it.
15. It is never clear who is to do what or when.

16. The planning approver is not knowledgeable or is disinterested.
17. We plan only after a problem has become acute.
18. The plan is never followed up.
19. Nobody respects the abilities of the planners.
20. Past plans were too optimistic.
21. Goals are too ambitious.
22. People resist any plan.
23. Premature implementation
24. If the plan doesn't show an immediate dollar return, it hasn't a chance.
25. Planning is not coordinated; others are doing similar planning.
26. There's no point to planning; too many unforeseen things are beyond my control or vision.
27. If I commit myself, I will be held accountable.
28. The boss and the organization shoot from the hip; should I?
29. I don't have the authority to implement my planning.

*8. Plan from strengths to weaknesses.* Often, it becomes more natural to try it the other way. Schaller and Tidwell explain it this way.[5] A hypothetical church was bemoaning its condition and wanting to make some changes. Noting the absence of young couples, the conversation between two church leaders went something like this.

"You're right, Martha," agreed another older leader. "We do a pretty good job here at Ebenezer for couples in their fifties and sixties, but there is no future for our church in that age group. There's no question but that reaching out to young couples should be our top priority."

"I couldn't agree with you both more," added a man who was generally recognized to be the most influential leader at

Ebenezer Church. "I know it's easy to list a lot of other problems we have here. The Sunday School is down to a handful of kids, we're hurting financially, we need more parking, and we're short of leaders; but those are really symptoms of a more basic problem. If two dozen young adults joined the congregation next Sunday, all of these other problems would soon disappear!"

This approach to planning, priority-setting, and decision making is not unusual. It is one of the most widely used planning models to be found in the churches. For the purposes of this discussion it can be identified as *planning from weakness.* Or, to be more specific this planning model appears to be based on the assumption that the best approach to planning is to identify that area of ministry in which our church is least effective, or that function of the church in which we as a congregation are weakest, and make it the number one priority. This means concentrating on that specialized area of ministry in which the resources are the fewest, past experiences will be least effective, and local skills are the scarcest. There may be other approaches which have a greater probability of failure than this planning-from-weakness model, but it is very difficult to name more than two or three. There may be other techniques which are more likely to undermine the morale of the congregation, but they are very rare. There may be other administrative processes which are more likely to be nonproductive, but they too are fortunately very rare.

9. *Plan for "Bad News at Flat Rock."* The poet has reminded us that the best laid plans of mice and men often go awry. Then what? Throw up our hands in futility and cry, "I knew it wouldn't work"? A far better option is to have an emergency plan already in the files. Although you hope that no one will rain on your parade, you know better. When the forecast is for rain, you had better get out your umbrella.

In initial planning, write down the possible risks involved in each stage of the actions planned. Then make some notes on how to act in terms of such an emergency. Far better it is to act from planning than to blindly react from a crisis.

Emergency planning is like taking out fire insurance. If you do not use it, so much the better. If you need it, you have it. Perhaps we are all tempted to say that we only have fire insurance when we don't need it. Or, it must pay to worry because everything I worry about never happens. And we laugh about it, but subconsciously maybe we are considering cancelling the fire insurance for next year. Before you do, talk to someone who had a fire without insurance.

Obviously, we are not limiting this section to fire insurance. A fire can only burn down the church building. Other unforeseen emergencies can tear down the *church* itself. That is a crisis of real concern. If your planning has any boldness and imagination, it will also have some risk. Better be prepared with some emergency plans if the risks become too risky.

## A Case Study

In 1960, the Wieuca Road Baptist Church of Atlanta was only six years old. Good planning and administration had given the church an unusually good birth. There were 1,100 members with a budget of nearly $200,000. But the church had plateaued two years previously. The pastor, J. T. Ford, and other leaders of the church felt it was time to plan for another five-year cycle.

We met countless times after gathering data. In May 1961, our recommendations were presented to the congregation. After three sessions of discussion and refinement, the plan was adopted. Note the plans and the historical results. (Only a small portion of the plans are listed here.)

| Action Planned | Results |
|---|---|
| 1. Develop job descriptions for all personnel and committees by June 1961. | 1. Completed in June, 1961. |
| 2. Sponsor a mission in 1961. | 2. Mission started in 1961; became a church in 1962. Budget of former mission, $500,000 in 1978. |
| 3. Establish Family-Night Supper program on Wednesday by October, 1961. | 3. Began in October, 1961. Average 500 in attendance by 1968. |
| 4. Redesign and reactivate new member orientation class by 1962. | 4. Reactivated in 1962 and use continues in 1978. |
| 5. Develop membership profile by 1962. | 5. Kardex file instituted in 1962; computerized in 1969. |
| 6. Develop a camping program for children and youth by June, 1962. | 6. One-week camp for children and one for youth began in 1962. By 1967, more than 250 attending. |
| 7. Institute weekly teachers' meetings by October, 1962. | 7. Began in October, 1962. |
| 8. Strengthen missionary education for youth by doubling attendance by January, 1963. | 8. Strengthened existing girls' groups and established groups for boys in 1962. Total attendance increased by 80 percent, by March, 1963. |
| 9. Plan to occupy interim sanctuary in 1962, and permanent sanctuary in 1970. | 9. First services held in respective sanctuaries in July, 1962 and January, 1971. |

There were four objectives with twelve goals, and thirty-five tasks (actions). The church reached three objectives very well and one in a fair manner. Over 90 percent of the tasks were completed during the five-year plan. The members do not recall this time in the life of the church as one of great growth. (That came in the next five years.) But they do recognize these years as the time of foundation building.

# 4
# Decision Making

"Delay the tough decisions as long as possible . . . they may go away!"

*Decision is choosing between the alternatives available in order to accomplish the objective in the most effective way.*

## A Case Study

Jimmy Jones is a home missionary in the inner city. Prepared. Committed. A hard worker. He has a vision for the ministry of the mission center to change the lives of persons in the community. Several new programs have been instituted under his leadership. He appreciates the leadership of the association of churches and particularly Bob Martin, the director of missions.

Only one problem continually faces Jimmy: The mission center does not have enough funds to underwrite the program he has envisioned for the community. There is always too much month at the end of the money. When discussing this with Bob he found a willing listener, and sometimes Bob indicated to Jimmy that there was more money coming next year. However, this was primarily wishful thinking. The associational budget was a tight one. Not only was there no "fat" in it, but sometimes a few "bones" were missing.

Jimmy mistook Bob's concern to mean approval to purchase some much needed items. One day a bill for $325 was received at the associational office for some recreational equip-

65

ment. It put Bob in a bind to dig up enough new money to cover the unexpected (and unbudgeted) purchase. He weathered the crisis and decided not to counsel with Jimmy about the seriousness of such irresponsible actions. Why cause a stir for $325? The equipment was badly needed.

In a few weeks Jimmy spent another $265 for a used motion picture projector. This was almost the straw that broke Bob's back, since the associational office had a good projecter that was under-used. The frustration level of both men continued to rise.

A few months later Jimmy asked Bob for permission to buy a new food freezer to replace the worn-out freezer. Bob knew there was a need, but there was no money available at that time. He considered the possibility of presenting the need to the missions committees of several churches. Before he could present his logic to the committees, the office received a bill for $705 for a new freezer. You guessed it . . . Jimmy had bought one.

Bob was beside himself. Something had to be done immediately. He telephoned his supervisor to get some advice. ("Advice" meaning permission to overspend his budget.) While sympathetic with the problem, the supervisor could not approve the overspending.

Bob finally decided to bell the cat and talk through the whole problem of overspending with Jimmy. In the process he said that he really wanted to allow the overspending but his supervisor would not approve. He failed to get to the heart of the problem: Jimmy was somewhat irresponsible in his expenditures and budget control. What transpired was additional hassling and more frustration. Bob could not force himself to make a hard decision and put an end to the overspending.

Is it any wonder that Jimmy continues to overspend? And Bob continues to fret? Do you see some classic traps in this case? Could you rationalize some of them if you were Bob? What decisions would you have made if you were Bob? or Jimmy?

## Locating the Traps

- I'm called to serve the Lord not to make so many decisions.
- Decisions are easy if you have all the information.
- Refer the hard decisions to your supervisors since they have more experience.
- Delay a decision if you can until a crisis makes the options more obvious.
- The more responsible the position, the more decisions need to be made.
- Some administrators are not involved in decision making.
- Delay a decision until you are sure you are right.
- When in doubt, say yes. It is a positive approach.
- Good planning ensures good decisions.
- Resources generally determine your decisions.

**Major Trap**—*Delay the tough decisions as long as possible, they may go away. Sometimes things just seem to work out themselves. It takes so much emotion to make a tough decision. If I make a wrong decision, it affects morale.*

Religious leaders may be tempted at this point more than any other group. Human nature makes everyone tend to avoid hard decisions. But Christian leaders should be more sensitive and caring than others. Since most tough decisions will come as bad news to some people, there is the temptation to try to eliminate the possibility of disappointment by having no news.

The key indicator is that low morale is affected more often by delayed decisions than by negative decisions. A *morale prob-*

*lem* has been defined by Dr. James Hayes as a conflict between a personal objective long-nourished and a management decision long-delayed. In discussing this concept in American Management Association seminars, he gives the following illustration.

While preparing to go on a family outing, he was careful to avoid making the other members unhappy by deciding where they would drive. So he asked them where they would like to go for a Saturday's outing. Each one indicated they did not care. But he knew that the son wanted to go to the beach. The daughter wanted to visit the museum. His wife needed to visit the shopping center. He just wanted to get out of the house, so any of the three alternatives were acceptable to him.

As they backed out of the driveway, each member of the family had a personal objective for the day. Yet, they did not want to impose their choice upon the other family members. In order to go to any one of the three destinations, they would normally drive to a common intersection. As the car moved towards the unknown destination of the day, each member was thinking "I hope . . . I hope . . . I hope." The nearer to the intersection they got, they began to think, "We must . . . We must . . . We must!" Everyone was happy, until Jim turned at the intersection towards the beach. The son smiled and thought, great. The female contingent frowned, and thought, phooey. Jim gritted his teeth and uttered, "Why did I wait so long to make the decision?" It was a case of a personal objective long-nourished and a management decision long-delayed. He had a morale problem on his hands because of delaying the decision and raising the hopes of each member. Jim says his family is reasonable and would not have fretted if they had known before getting into the car that they were going to a destination other than their first choice.

**Other traps**—*1. More information makes it easy to make hard decisions. All I need is the facts. Once I have them, it is only a matter of weighing them and using common sense.* Sounds logical, doesn't it? As in most administrative traps, it has some truth to it, just enough to lead you on until you are at the bottom looking up.

Television detective, Jack Webb, coined the phrase, "The facts, ma'am. Just give me the facts." Let us look at what some others, more qualified to speak to us than the *Dragnet* detective, have to say. Henry Clay said, "Statistics are no substitute for judgment." For the Christian approach, Fulton Oursler said, "In making our decisions, we must use the brains that God has given us. But we must also use our hearts which He also gave us." Surely, when the moment of decision comes for the Christian, there are more reflections to be made than from the mind only. What about the heart? The Spirit? Faith goes beyond reason.

How then do the facts help us? They help us make *better* decisions. No computer, even a sophisticated one, can ever make a decision. They affect the quality of the matter. Hard decisions are never easy to make. (Soft decisions are easy to make.) Tough decisions come out of loving, disciplined emotions. It is the will that motivates us to follow through to the best conclusion on the weightier decisions of life.

*2. Executives make the most decisions. After all, they are the most experienced. That's what they are paid to do. They make policy. I do the work. Don't bother me with decisions.* Sound familiar? From either pole, it has a validity. The truth is that the more responsible the position, the fewer decisions to be made.

Consider the anecdote of the husband who says, "I make the major decisions of our family. My wife makes the minor ones. She decides the smaller things; car purchase, house location and decoration, and family budgeting. I decide how we react to the national debt, foreign trade, and ecology."

Executives of multimillion dollar conglomerates are expected to make only a few decisions a month. Naturally, these decisions are of far-reaching consequences. The first-line managers may make ten decisions a day of a much easier magnitude.

Decisions need to be delegated even more than tasks. The decisions then pyramid towards the top when the chief executive takes the accumulation of input and mulls over his decision as long as necessary to make a good choice. Syrus, the Roman philosopher, said, "That should be considered long, which can be decided only once."

Administration requires decision making. A state executive director may be deciding on the merits of recommending the purchase of a two-million-dollar conference facility. A mission pastor may be choosing between two dozen chairs at $5.95 each. Both are administrators making decisions.

*3. The best decision-maker is the boss. He has the wider view. He might as well make it now because he is going to review my decision anyway.* This is a first cousin to the former trap and deals with similar logic and consequences.

The fact is, usually the boss cannot always make the best decision. He is too far removed from the scene of the action. He just does not know what is going on at that point. If he did, he probably would not be able to understand and interpret it in the light of the decision.

Consider the decision to be made on the height of the windows in the Children's Division of the new educational building. The pastor and the architect may agree that all windows should be a certain height from the floor to give symmetry from the outside. The minister of education may have specialized in youth and adult work and readily agrees that the standard height is obviously the proper choice.

But what about the lady who works with the small children? What does she think? The pastor might well ask, Does it make any difference? Aren't windows all at the same height? Why not ask her? She works in that area. It may flatter her to be given the opportunity to agree. And what does she say? Windowsills should be considerably lower for small children, so they can see outdoors.

Decisions should be made at the point nearest the action. Good choices are made at the level which will help ensure good decisions at the executive level, not to mention the confidence it gives to the people on the local scene.

*4. Decisions are best made at the moment of crisis. It is only then that most of the facts surface. The pressure of the moment will motivate decisiveness.*

The best decisions come prior to a crisis and can be decided without the pressure of deadlines and emotion. The word *crisis* dictates urgency and maybe the decision requires additional information and time for reflecting upon the options available. Decisions do not demand snap judgments. Rather, they accrue gradually to the moment of decision.

When the energy crisis of 1974, coupled with the inflation-recession crisis, brought almost every organization to their knees, some prayed, some pleaded, some lost their furniture to the lending agency. The organizations that were least affected were those who had made some decisions prior to the crisis.

I recall the services section at the Home Mission Board spending considerable time in a "business game": What would we do if our income were reduced by 10 percent tomorrow? Not only was it a helpful exercise in emergency budgeting, but it gave us some good decisions made without stress and pressure. Since we were not faced with a severe reduction in income, was it worth the time? You decide. We had an emergency plan in the files that could be activated at any moment. It provided a reappraisal of our budget priorities. It was management insurance against poor decisions. Yes, Virginia, necessity is still the mother of invention!

5. *Refer all tough decisions to your supervisor. Let him decide for you. His position gives the perspective.* This is a spin-off of the second trap listed. Its uniqueness is only the difficult choices tend to be referred to your supervisor.

Stop and think about the decisions you made last month. There were some enjoyable ones. You were glad to make those. They made others happy as well as yourself. Some decisions were harder to make, but you wanted to have control over the outcome, so you were glad to wear the hat of decision-maker.

Here comes a trap. Here is a decision that you know should be a no response. But you do not want to make the requestor unhappy, so you refer it to your supervisor. Is that fair? Your supervisor has enough decisions to make. Why increase his load with a decision that rightfully belongs to you? Besides, if he must make all of your decisions, why does he need you on the management team?

Beware! There is a natural temptation to want to say yes to the requestor when you know the answer should be no. Whatever you do, do not get caught in the trap of telling your supervisee, "I felt the decision should have been yes, but I referred it to my supervisor and he said, no." That really puts your boss in a bad light. After all, you should have made the no decision and had the courage to administer it.

6. *Goal setting and budgeting are necessary evils. I want to spend my time working with people and not shuffling papers on a desk. Somebody else can make those theoretical decisions. I prefer to make mine with life and blood situations.* This is a related trap to those found in chapters 1 and 2. But it has some specific applications.

Goals and budgets are road maps toward your organizational or personal objective. They are tools in getting your job done easier and better. Without them you are likely to expend a lot of energy going the wrong direction and not even approaching your objective.

Turning your back on these management tools will limit your effectiveness. It is almost like entering a race with a millstone about your neck. Financial resources are usually important in attaining your objective. Why be caught without enough funds or with misdirected funds? A little planning and careful, priority budgeting could be very helpful.

The person-oriented administrator will quickly learn that more persons can be helped in the long run by setting goals and budgets in priority fashion.

You may hear some persuasive administrators talk about putting enough fat in their budget requests for safety's sake. They say it is always better to have allowed for income shrinkage by padding your expense requests. Their motto might be: Good budgeting, like prime beef, will include a gracious amount of fat. But wait a few years until the record shows they have annually fattened up their requests. Not only do they personally suffer but also their work must suffer for their administrative sins.

## Questionnaire

Before reading the section on how to avoid the traps, test yourself. Maybe the foregoing rhetoric has not focused on a specific situation. Judge your actions of the last few years.

True     False

| | | |
|---|---|---|
| _____ | _____ | I tend to avoid decisions when possible. |
| _____ | _____ | Basically, I feel if I have all the information, the decision can easily be made. |

_____ _____ The emotion of the moment plays into my decisions.

_____ _____ I wish I were the boss so I wouldn't have to bother with decision making.

_____ _____ I tend to give positive decisions because I do not like to disappoint people.

_____ _____ I will avoid taking risks at almost any cost.

_____ _____ I always expect good decisions from subordinates.

_____ _____ I try to be decisive.

_____ _____ I try to be incisive.

_____ _____ My philosophy is, You win a few and you lose a few.

_____ _____ All decisions should be made before night falls.

_____ _____ I seek the advice of others when the decision falls outside my field of expertise.

_____ _____ Generally, resources are now more determined by decisions than vice versa.

## How to Avoid Decision Making Traps

There are countless quotations available that would serve as a guide to avoid traps. Perhaps Chester Bowles gave as good advice as any when he said, "When you approach a (decision), strip yourself of preconceived opinions and prejudice, assemble and learn the facts of the situation, make the decision which seems to you to be the most honest, and then stick to it."

One of the most stimulating declarations of *Future Shock* was the dramatic change in the relationship of decision to resources. Generally in the past, resources determined decisions. We counted our assets and then decided which course to take. Tofler predicts that the future will demand of us to make good decisions that will generate adequate resources to make greater decisions. This should catch the eye of the Christian church. Of all organizations in the world, we should be willing to make decisions on faith, regardless of the financial and human resources available.

Historically, the church has moved on the shoulders of decision. Think of the landmark decisions made by Jesus, Paul, the Antioch church, the Council of Nicaea, Martin Luther, Roger Williams, and countless recent and contemporary leaders.

**General Guidelines—***1. An administrator is a person who decides—sometimes right, sometimes wrong.* Decisiveness is a part of his character. A good administrator decides right more times than wrong. Decisiveness and wisdom are a part of his makeup. Since few decisions are final, you have the option of making a later decision to refine a poor one.

*2. The person who insists on making perfect decisions either never decides or suffers constant frustration.* H. W. Andrews puts it in perspective.

While an open mind is priceless, it is priceless only when its owner has the courage to make a final decision which closes the mind for action after the process of viewing all sides of the question has been completed. Failure to make a decision after due consideration of all the facts will quickly brand a man as unfit for a position of responsibility. Not all of your decisions will be correct. None of us is perfect. But if you get into the habit of making decisions, experience will develop your judgment to a point where more and more of your decisions will be right. After all, it is better to be right 51 % of the time and get something done, than it is to get nothing done because you fear to reach a decision.[1]

*3. Great decisions usually precipitate from a choice of alternatives, the best of the good or the least of the bad options that are available at the moment.* The question then comes,

Good for whom? for me? for you? for the group? for our objective? for the kingdom of God? Bad for whom and so forth. Maybe the first decision made is to decide on what needs to be decided.

4. *Conditions of certainty breed potentially bad decisions.* Kenneth E. Boulding writes in *Technology Review,*

Evaluation and decision strategy, and the quality of decisions in general, depend very much on degree of uncertainty of the items to be decided. The greater the uncertainty, the higher value which should be placed on decisions which leave future options open—that is, on noncommitment. Decision making under high degrees of uncertainty is a very different kind of beast from decision making under low degrees of uncertainty. Absolute certainty is unknown in the real world.

An important source of bad decisions is illusions of certainty, which often lead to decisive action which zeros in on disaster. Computerized and numerical models, especially those with fancy diagrams and printouts, are almost certain to produce illusions of certainty and may therefore lead to bad decisions.

When efficiency leads to a loss of adaptability, and information leads to illusions of certainty, and centralization leads to both of these, we have a magnificent design for extinction! [2]

5. *You are able to evaluate whether a decision is good or bad more in terms of months after D day, rather than in days after the decision.* It is more like interpreting history from a book than it is reading a current event in the newspaper.

6. *Making one good decision is worth a week's work.* Developing a good decision-maker is worth a year's work. This is a further refinement of the management principle of getting things done through other people. It is a paraphrase of the slogan of the sixties, "Give a man a fish and you have filled his stomach for a day. Teach him how to fish and you have filled his stomach for a life time." Trusting others with some of our decisions is most difficult. But it can be most rewarding.

*Trust* is a contagious word. To trust a person with your automobile provides him with encouragement. To trust him with your decision-making process is even a greater encouragement.

**Specific Guidelines**—*1. Understand what generally causes bad decisions.* This list was found in *Supervision.*[3]

- Lack of information—Insufficient facts lead to guessing, and a wrong guess may be disastrous.
- Lack of time—More time to get facts, to weigh and decide, increases the chance for a wise decision.
- Presence of emotion—Emotions are the main cause of bias; when emotion is stronger than reason, anything can happen.
- Presence of fear—Running scared often influences decisions adversely.
- Presence of risk—When risk is great, decisions may be overcautious and weak.
- Lack of attention—When a problem is not considered serious, it may be lightly passed off or ignored.
- Lack of authority—Responsibility without authority leads to soft, unenforceable decisions.
- Lack of skill in decision making—Some supervisors simply are not aware of how to go about making good decisions. Judgments are questioned most often when the background and reasoning which led to the decision are not clear.

*2. Understand what will help you make sound decisions.* Loen gives some helpful suggestions in *Manage More By Doing Less.*[4]

- "Tailor your decision-making methods to your personal strengths and weaknesses. As in everyone, you are a unique individual with certain innate characteristics and with a combination of knowledge and experience. You have certain strengths and weaknesses." This helps to explain why a genius in one field may be a complete flop in another. Henry Ford, for example, was an engineering genius, but his management methods almost ruined his company.

- "Make sure your decision is needed." If it will not have a significant impact upon the success or failure of your operation, you should try to delegate it.
- "Identify the right problems." Try to make sure that you are dealing with the real cause of your problem.
- "Use a decision-making method that fits your problem. Don't swat a fly with a sledge hammer."

   3. *Understand and be familiar with tested method of decision making.* Charles H. Kepner, social psychiatrist, and Benjamin B. Tregoe, sociologist, specializing in management training, have developed the following sequence of procedures.[5]

- The objectives of a decision must be established first.
- The objectives are classified as to importance.
- Alternative actions are developed.
- The alternatives are evaluated against the established objectives.
- The choice of the alternatives best able to achieve all the objectives represents the tentative decision.
- The tentative decision is explored for future possible adverse consequences.
- The effects of the final decision are controlled by taking other actions to prevent possible adverse consequences from becoming problems, and by making sure the actions decided on are carried out.

   4. *Make minor decisions as soon as possible and relieve your mind and emotions of those decisions.* This will provide you additional strength to make your major decisions. When possible make decisions now, for they can be reviewed later. The moment a decision comes to your attention, see yourself grabbing hold and struggling with it and finally disposing it. Golf pros say that you should envision the flight of the ball

before you address the shot. Thus you learn to be the decider and not the procrastinator.

5. *Every decision, if broken down into small, bite sizes, will be easier to make.* This is a simplification of the overwhelming complexity of the massive computer. Bit-by-bit and bite-by-bite it accumulates information until it has reams of paper to spit out its findings.

6. *"When pressed into a decision, it is always better to say no than yes. It is easier to change a no to a yes than vice versa."* This advice was given by a veteran vice-president of AT&T while serving on the church council. At the time, I thought it quite conservative. In the fifteen years that have passed, it has changed from conservative to wise.

Dr. Arthur B. Rutledge had a similar philosophy for timing in decision making. He often would counsel that it is better to wait for a yes answer, than to press for an immediate answer and get a no.

Charles Hole expressed it this way, "Deliberate with caution, but act with decisiveness; yield with graciousness, or oppose with firmness."

7. *The price of indecision is usually a heavy one.* H. A. Hopf put it eloquently. "Indecision is debilitating; it feeds upon itself. It is, one might say, habit-forming. Not only that, but it is contagious. It transmits itself to others. Often greater risk is involved in postponement than in making a wrong decision."

John Foster expressed a similar feeling. "Nothing can be more destructive to vigor of action than protracted, anxious fluctuation, through resolutions adopted, rejected, resumed, suspended, and nothing causes a greater expense of feeling. A man without decision can never be said to belong to himself. He is as a wave of the sea, or a feather in the air which every breeze blows about as it listeth."

What these Englishmen are saying is that leaders had better make up their minds and get with it. When it is your time at bat, you have to go up and take your swings.

8. *A group decision is usually a better decision.* It is generally a safer one. The process takes longer because of group input and the emotions to be considered after a group member has authored an unacceptable idea. However, in decisions of far-reaching consequences, it is usually the better part of wisdom to get as many divergent ideas as possible before decision time. It is one thing for your associates to have the knowledge that you heard them, and still you did not choose their recommendation. It is another thing for them to feel they were not heard at all. Or, to paraphrase, it is better to have given input and lost, than to have never had input at all.

9. *A word about zero-base budgeting (ZBB).* Since decision making is the key to budgeting, it might be helpful to look briefly at the philosophy of the newest style. President Carter did not discover ZBB. (My wife says that we have been practicing ZBB since we were married. The only difference is that we seem to start *and* finish with zero.)

It is based upon the premise that nothing is set in concrete when you begin to plan next year's budget. The use of the word *zero* is a bit misleading in the manner in which most corporations utilize the concept. In the sense that every line item for budgeting should be evaluated for inclusion or exclusion, *zero* is an appropriate term.

As the concept is practiced, the organization considers if the program is worth continuing at all. If not, it is discarded and budgeted zero. If it has worth, it is given consideration of *how worthy when compared with every other recommendation* for the new year. This puts every program in competition for a slice of the budget on a priority basis. This is a radical change from the way most religious organizations budget.

## A Case Study

While on a Bold Mission Thrust project last summer, a case of decision making surfaced while visiting a mission church in Chicago. The congregation had exhibited very little growth, with attendance averaging about forty. The only consistency seemed to be the leaky roof that functioned every time it rained.

The pastor reported the problem at a regular business meeting and said that it could be fixed for three hundred dollars. The church had almost no money and refused to practice deficit spending. They debated for six months what they would do about the roof, in addition to moving the pots each time it rained to collect the water.

There still was no money. The pastor finally decided on his own to authorize the new roof. The roofers came, the leaking was stopped, and to the amazement of everyone more than three hundred dollars was collected the following week from the congregation.

An actual example of the futuristic principle that good decisions determine resources. The pastor testified that this physical improvement was a spiritual lift to the congregation. It gave them new confidence that they could reach a church-wide objective.

# 5
# Delegating

*Delegating is the distribution of work and authority in such a manner that associate's skills will best be utilized in terms of reaching your objective.*

## A Case Study

Max is a good planner and even a better decision-maker. His ministry is characterized by careful forecasting, objectifying, evaluation, and deciding. Nobody, not even a PhD in business management, could score against Max's precept and practice in these areas.

Then why is it that the fruits of his ministry seem to plateau-out after about three years as the leader of an organized church?

The truth of the matter is that Max cannot delegate well if at all. He cannot remedy this malady because he is not even aware of this deficiency. Even a physician cannot prescribe for something that he cannot diagnose.

Let's have a retake of Max's handling of a specific problem he faced in his church. See if you can locate the traps he failed to recognize. Perhaps you might underline them as you read this case study.

The Valley View Baptist Church had a resident membership of 450, in a newly developed community. The budget was $90,000. The building debt retirement payments swallowed up most of the remaining funds after salaries, missions and basic operating expenses. The staff consisted of Max, a secretary, and a custodian.

The pastor's planning and decision-making processes determined that teacher training was vital to growing their church. The educational force was ready and willing but obviously not able.

Max concluded that this priority item must claim his time and energy. But where was he going to get the time when he already felt he was giving 110 percent? Wrestling with the impasse, he decided that importance demanded that he teach the leadership course himself.

Within one month his sensory-emotional system cried out, No way! But the need remained. So Max decided to delegate this responsibility to a volunteer. He wanted a person to whom he could turn over the responsibility for teacher training. If I could only wash my hands of the whole package! Besides that, I don't need to spend that amount of energy for so small a group. But if I delegate this responsibility . . . will I lose control? he wondered.

But to whom should I delegate? The only qualified person is Suzie Jones. (A recently retired teacher at the local junior college.) But she cannot relate to these teachers-in-training. She's too old to lead our young adult leadership. She taught English to youth. What does she know about biblical pedagogy?

To make a long story disastrous, Max finally chose Suzie because he had no other alternative. He gave her a briefing and she eagerly accepted the task. He told her what he had planned to do and directed her to follow his well thought through plan. And thus the training work was delegated.

Suzie found the pastor's plan to be insufficient for reaching his stated objective. It was also incompatible with her knowledge, experience, and teaching style. When she communicated this to Max, he politely, but firmly, explained to her that his methods were time-honored through the seminaries and had been practical for him in the past.

She persisted another two months. Teachers became disinterested. Suzie became disillusioned. Max became frustrated. He unknowingly pronounced the last rites of the training program. He intoned, "Well, I always knew that volunteers were not worth the time it takes for supervision. If the training program is important, I guess I must find time to do it myself."

The cycle was complete. But the task had not been achieved.

## Locating the Traps

- If it is to be, it is to be by me.
- I have too much responsibility, so I'll delegate some of it.
- I'll delegate some things: those I don't want to do; those I don't know how to do.
- Delegate methods to be sure it is done your way.
- Don't give authority to the very young, the aging, and especially to women.
- Volunteers are not worth the supervision they need.
- Delegation is too risky. I lose control.

**Major Trap**—*If you want a thing done right, do it yourself. How many times have I asked others to help out, only to find they did a subpar job or did not follow through at all? The stakes are too high to risk my important work with others less experienced and less qualified. If it means I have to work eighty hours a week, I'll pay the price.*

Everyone of us has spent some time in this trap. The temptation to overevaluate our skills and commitment is always an ego temptation for leaders. To complicate matters, we tend to underappreciate the potential of our associates. This is a good time to remember the strategy of our Lord. Where would the Christian movement be if he had felt it necessary to do everything himself? Where would we be? When we compare our spiritual abilities and capabilities with those of Jesus, we pale by comparison.

After that remorseful comparison, we go right out and assess our associates as incompetent to carry a part of the load. How odd!

There is a fine line between the following statements. See if you can draw the line in your mind. "If it is to be, it is to be by me." (Often called the eleven deadly two-lettered words.) "If it is to be, it is up to me." A case could be made for either statement. Can they both be right? Yes, if you see the distinction. The first statement deals with the *action;* the second deals with *responsibility.* The former is the trap that says that everything to be done needs to be done by me. The latter realizes that once a responsibility has been given (and accepted), it is up to me to see that it is done—by me or maybe, better done by someone else.

The major concern of the corporate world today is called the Crisis of Middle Management. A company has many competent people serving in middle management positions who are frustrated because they do not have work to challenge them. Upper management tends to withhold delegation of authority. Lower management sits on their hands waiting for leadership. Is this the case in your organization? If so, give careful reading to the rest of the chapter. The effectiveness and perhaps the life of your organization may be at stake, not to mention your effectiveness as a leader.

The construction of this trap is based on the foundation of the question posed in chapter 2: Are you a doer or a manager? You can be a leader in either case. However, the manager delegates and multiplies his effectiveness.

**Other Traps**—*1. You can delegate responsibility. When your load gets too heavy and the strain is almost unbearable, find some person to whom you can delegate some of your responsibility.*

This temptation is wide and deep, confusing enough to be a hazardous trap. There are two principles in delegation that become intertwined, making the trap. First, you can delegate authority, but not responsibility. A higher authority has given you the responsibility and you have accepted it. If the task is not done, you are still responsible, regardless of whether you delegated it to someone else or not.

Consider the captain of a ship. He is given the command of the vessel and all the responsibility that goes with it. He delegates his authority to several officers for execution. Ultimately, he is responsible to see that they function acceptably. Even though the captain is not on the bridge of the ship giving directions for its steering, he is held responsible for running aground or a collision. The captain could delegate his authority to the officer of the deck for steering. But he could not delegate his responsibility in case of disaster.

Second, you should not delegate a task without giving appropriate authority to the person accepting the task. Some religious leaders find this difficult. When you pass on some authority, you give up some of your power. Often, we do not mind living without abundant financial resources. But do not try to strip us of our power! History has shown that most of the great leaders of the world have placed a higher priority on power than on wealth. Yet, it is the sharing of the power (authority) that we extend our ability to achieve our objective.

Jesus and his Spirit have been trying to convince his followers of this fact for two thousand years.

When you do delegate your authority to another, remember he then becomes a manager also. Perhaps he will further delegate a portion of the assignment to others. At that point, you cease to be the supervisor of the "others." They will be supervised by the person who subdelegated that portion of work to them. No man can be supervised by two masters. Not only might he love the one and hate the other, but also he may grow to hate them both. He may decline or resign. You have lost a worthy associate or two worthy associates. When you delegate, give away everything except your responsibility.

2. *Volunteerism is a good idea, but it is not practical. It takes more time to enlist volunteers, match their skills with your needs, and supervise them than it is worth.*

What one of us has not experienced the above frustration? It is one thing to be frustrated. It is another thing to allow that emotion to ensnare you into a trap. The principle has worked for centuries. Why desert it now? Jesus called for volunteers for his disciples. He named twelve of them as apostles. They called forth volunteers to lead the early church. Bishops, elders, and pastors were all called for volunteer service to help in the work of the kingdom.

Stop a minute! Where would your spiritual pilgrimage have ceased if there were not volunteers to make a contribution to your life? Where would your organization be without the help of volunteers? Most of us would have to restrict severely our outreach. Some would have to close up the shop. So, let's not throw out the baby with the bath. Or, to keep our metaphor consistent, let's not jump into the trap just because we see that some volunteer movements have failed.

The Home Mission Board, where I work, determined its

objectives for the next decade to be: "Let every person in our land have an opportunity to hear and accept the gospel of Jesus Christ; let every person in our land have an opportunity to share in the witness and ministry of a New Testament fellowship of believers." When considering the challenge of such dramatic objectives, the leadership considered the assets available compared to the assets needed to reach these objectives. When counting only full-time paid missionaires and ministers, the objectives were unreasonable and unreachable. Only when the use of hundreds of thousands of volunteers were considered were the objectives within reason.

*3. Youth, women, minority groups, and senior citizens should not be delegated much authority. Remember the counsel of our forefathers, "Don't send a boy to do a man's work." The Christian church has marched forward on the shoulders of mature male leaders in the past.*

In our modern society you would think that this trap would catch only the people trying to hang on to those "good old days" of the nineteenth century. Actually, there seems to be a waiting line to jump in. As a fact, there are barriers and signs all about the trap warning the administrator to beware. There is the sign of history, of practicality, of freedom, of individual rights, of common sense, of supply and demand, and of effectiveness. There are barriers of Satan urging us to be restrictive in our leadership and administrative roles. And yet, the male role and image is so strong (often bullheaded) that a man refuses to read the signs, jumps over the barriers, and falls head over heels into the trap.

Consider each of these categories. First, youth. The apostles were at most in their younger twenties. Presidents of major corporations and educational institutions are younger than the average age of the leadership in our churches. In some churches you have to be older to serve as a deacon than John Kennedy was to be elected president of the United States. Youth have the zeal and the education to accept heavy assignments in the kingdom. They have our intellectual assent and our emotional encouragement. What we fail to give them is our confidence and our spiritual blessings. Is it right for them to be allowed to play church during youth week once a year and not be allowed to offer their lives in committed and continued service?

Second, women. I would not try to be convincing based upon logic or theology. Others more qualified than I have often failed. My appeal would assume Christian precepts but would be made upon practicality. Respond to the following statements with your own true-or-false answer. In the last thirty years, women members outnumber the men in your church. Women have more positions of service in your church today than do men. Women are usually more willing to serve than men when asked. Women usually can give more time to the task. Women tend to be more spiritually discerning.

Like it or not, I must answer true to all five statements. For most churches, the statistics and performances will bear out such a true response. Then, why is it that we still persist in trying to enlist some average men for positions of service when we have some outstanding women waiting on the sidelines? I am afraid that I know the answer and do not want to see it in print.

But have we considered the reality of what our God must think of our judgment? Are we being good stewards of the most precious of his resources, his own children? It is one thing not to put our money to work for God. It must be a graver mistake not to put his children to work for him.

Third, minority groups. We tend to trap ourselves with all of the preceding prejudices when we think of the possibilities for persons from minority groups, plus a few more. The largest of these is to assume that other cultures do not have a significant role to play in extending the kingdom of God. This reminds us of the limerick that begins with: "How odd of God, to choose the Jews." If we claim that minorities lack in culture, we had better step back and reassess that statement. They may lack in our terms of culture but not in terms of their concept of culture.

We have learned of the skills and abilities of black persons in athletic endeavors. Is it possible we have overlooked their contribution to the greatest field of competition: the eternal fight against evil? In the last twenty years most Anglo churches have adopted some of the more informal characteristics of the black church at worship. Are there other undiscovered gifts of leadership that are going untapped because of our reluctance to take the risk of delegation?

Fourth, senior citizens. By now, you should be able to write this section yourself. Many of these persons have the qualities we seek for responsibility and leadership: experience, maturity, financial resources, time, commitment, and desire to be involved. Why then are we not delegating more authority to them? Could it be that young and middle-aged adults have traditionally put their seniors on the shelf as over the hill at sixty-five?

The facts indicate that the largest potential for effective volunteers is represented by persons sixty years and older. Early retirement and affluence has opened up this personnel market. Second vocations, usually beginning in middle age, gives people an opportunity to do some things they have always dreamed of doing. They can accept a lower salary or do volunteer work on the side.

*4. Delegate matters that you do not like to do or are not comfortable in doing. Let a subordinate do those things. That's one of the few compensations in being the boss. Anyway, that*

*saves energy to do the important matters. And besides, you
can't be good at everything.*

This is an example of some good management logic, confused and confounded in the midst of some sorry rationalizing.
Surely, no one can excel in everything. Managers cannot get
involved in small decisions and activities. The work needs to
be distributed, and the manager is the logical one to make
the division among his associates. It is the mixture of this uncon-
tested logic that makes the trap unnoticed, even attractive.

The point is that considering the above truths as givens,
administrators should avoid delegating tasks that are rightfully
theirs to do. If it carries executive responsibility, an associate
or volunteer is probably not equipped to handle it. This is
known as forced delegation or overdelegating. It is especially
dangerous to delegate a task that you personally dislike. Unless,
it requires a skill that you do not have. Even in that event,
you should consider if you need to learn that skill in order to
have control in your responsibilities. If you dislike it, the
chances are poor that someone else will desire it. The emotional
risks are high in delegating an unwanted assignment. The delegatee may assume that the manager keeps all the good apples
and gives out only the rotten ones.

Perhaps the most subtle aspect is wanting to delegate work
that you are not comfortable in doing. Maybe you are inexperi-
enced in that field or have not enjoyed much success in the
past. So why not delegate it? Mainly, because you lose control.
Until you know firsthand about that facet of the work, how
do you expect to be in control of assuring its fulfillment? Until
you have done the work of candy keeper, how will you know
where others are hiding the candy?

Once you have done and understand the work of the candy
keeper, you can delegate that task simply because you have
control over the process. You know where the candy can be

hidden. You may have hidden it yourself. By that very fact, you are in control. You can counsel with the delegatee and help him to do the task that will help meet the group's objective.

## Questionnaire

Why not check yourself at this point to see how you are measuring up as a delegator?

| Yes | No | |
|---|---|---|
| _____ | _____ | 1. Am I willing to delegate work that I enjoy (but may be left undone) to others? |
| _____ | _____ | 2. Do I allow them to do it differently than the way I would do it? |
| _____ | _____ | 3. Would I accept the fact they may make mistakes, even fail? |
| _____ | _____ | 4. Is it more important to gain my organization's objective than to relinquish some of my authority and power? |
| _____ | _____ | 5. Do I see delegation as being risky? |
| _____ | _____ | 6. If wisely delegated, is it usually worth the risk? |
| _____ | _____ | 7. Do I have more work to do than I can get done? |
| _____ | _____ | 8. Are there potential delegatees in my organization? |
| _____ | _____ | 9. With training, could they perform the task well? |
| _____ | _____ | 10. Do I know why I am not delegating more of my tasks? |

## How to Avoid the Delegation Trap

**General Guidelines**—*1. Delegating to groups is a whole new ball game.* Individuals are easier to supervise. Groups have many and diverse opinions. You can call an associate into your office and explain the facts to him, and thus divert his errant ways. But a group is different. There may not even be enough chairs in your office to seat them.

Groups do not make decisions in structured organizations. You may say that your organization is not structured. Not from your viewpoint, maybe, but have you asked any of your associates or members what they think? Groups do research and make suggestions. They carry out decisions delegated to them by a person. You still think groups make decisions? Then why is it when a group makes a bad decision, a specific person gets the blame for it? Decision goes with responsibility and responsibility goes with individuals.

Then why delegate to groups? Because most tasks do not require decision making. The policy is already set. The group's job is to carry out the task within the guidelines of the policy. In the ecclesiastical world, there are countless tasks that can be done effectively in groups.

(1) *Committees.* Much has been said about committees. Very little is neutral. Fun and jibes have been tossed at committee work. Some have said that is only a way of postponing a decision. Others have said that a camel is a horse created by a committee. My experience leads me to conclude that a committee can design a horse with the stamina of a camel.

The success or failure of committee work (or any other group work) is determined by the directions given by the delegator. Specific instructions should be given regarding the objective of the committee, guidelines for action, and a dateline for completion. Progress reports should be expected at critical times. If the work needs continuing, make sure the members understand the current objective. Disband the committee when the objective has been achieved.

Specific examples of the use of committees are given at the end of this chapter.

(2) *Ad-hocracy.* Alvin Toffler made this coined term popular in his book, *Future Shock.* It means a committee organized for a one-time task. A first cousin of the standing committee, it may be more efficient. It has the advantage of being constituted for one purpose only, at one time only. Members with specific expertise can be appointed or co-opted for limited service.

(3) *Task Forces.* Primarily, the same as ad hoc groups, task forces usually cross organizational lines. The same traps lurk here as in the other small-group work.

*2. Consider why you may be having problems delegating.* If you know why you cannot easily delegate, you are halfway toward solving your problem.

- It takes too much of my time. It is easier to do it myself than to explain it to another person and then have to supervise them.
- My people are already overworked. It would only be shifting my overload to them.
- They won't accept the task seriously.
- I want it done right. Mistakes can be costly.
- My office carries clout, and I can get it done faster.
- Who will control the job if I delegate it?
- The task is too confidential to assign it.
- It is just too risky.

What do all of these add up to? Basically, the manager has problems delegating because he feels that the job can be done better by him. What he forgets to appraise is the long-run question: Can he continue to do well the other tasks assigned to him if he does not delegate other tasks that come along?

**Specific Guidelines—***1. Evaluate the human resources of your organization just as you do your financial resources.* If you know the potential of your people, you will be able to delegate more to their pleasure and to your profit as a leader.

Small organizations may be able to keep track of such human resources with a 3 by 5 card. Large organizations and churches often must rely upon some form of electronic data processing. in 1968 Wieuca Road Baptist Church transferred their membership profile records to data processing. Each member had an opportunity to record his experience and preference for service, including 144 options. There was no way this large congregation could have delegated its task among the congregation without a system for appraisal of their human resources.

*2. Recognize there are others just as talented and committed as you are to the objectives of your organization.* Not to do so, places you in an uncomfortable position of judgment.

*3. Survey what your organization is not achieving in terms of your objective.* Then reassign some of the work of the overload to those whose shoulders can take some bending. We might be surprised how many organizations already have available personnel to accomplish their objectives. But, usually, the organization needs to be rearranged and the work reassigned.

*4. Do you have confidence in your people?* If so, then you probably are willing to delegate. Do you trust them? If so, grant them the same opportunity to make the same number of mistakes you make. If you cannot trust persons, then do not risk delegating some of your authority. It will only bring you ulcers. (Maybe you can tolerate ulcers.) But it will also bring you failure to reach your objective. (Can you tolerate failure over the long haul?)

*5. Take advantage of the economic principle of* THE DIVISION OF LABOR. This concept has withstood the critique of all major economic systems of the world. Everyone of them from capitalism to Communism wants to get things done. They have specific objectives. Likewise, each system utilizes the division of labor principle. Secular philosophies do not have exclusive rights to this advantageous manner of effectively sharing the work to be done.

You may ask, "How do I divide the work among myself? I have no associates." If not, why not? Only hermits have no one to assist them. Many of us have a spouse. All of us have people helping us in reaching our objectives, hopefully, many types of volunteers. Give serious thought (approaching wisdom) to matching the needs of the task to the talents of your team. Assume there are eight tasks to be accomplished if your goal is to be reached. They might be diagrammed like this.

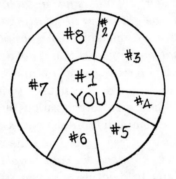

Note that you have decided to take task #1, which includes supervising the other seven persons (tasks). Without these delegatees, you might have been able to perform tasks #1, 2, 3, and 4, very well. Or, you might have done all eight very poorly.

In simplified language, division of labor entails discovering how many tasks need to be done; discovering persons who can help achieve the tasks; matching the round pegs with the round holes.

*6. Be willing to take risks, with discretion.* Most of the great advances in our society have begun with a risk element.

You may win a few and lose a few. But your wins probably will be more significant. And you may be surprised how soon you will forget the losses.

A word of caution about the "boat rockers." You really do not need helpers who are afraid to rock the boat. They will jump overboard at the first hint of a rough sea. The occasional boat rocker will keep a healthy tension among all those aboard.

However, you need to be wary of the perennial boat rockers. They tend to be more interested in causing tension and shock for the thrill of watching the insecurity of the group. They eventually will cause so much commotion that the whole group will get motion sickness. That tends to bring on sickness of the whole body, and that generally means physical and emotional expulsion and revulsion.

As a rule of thumb, take the risk of the boat rockers. It is easier to tame a wildcat than to arouse a Rip van Winkle.

## Examples of Delegating

One simple and one complex example may indicate the range of delegation in a local church. First, bulletin boards. For years the hallway boards, intended to communicate an organization's message to the church, were either poorly used, overused, or not used at all. Sometimes there was some competition and a sense of possessiveness.

Enter delegation. Assign every hallway board to a specific organization(s) of the church on a monthly schedule. Equality is exercised by rotating the locations. Control is ensured by stating that each board would be examined monthly. If it were not being used effectively, it would be reassigned to another organization.

Second, deacons' family ministry program. You probably already know about this pastoral program. It is an excellent example of the pastor (manager) delegating a part of his authority to the diaconate. If you are acquainted with it, check your practice of it with the principles stated in this chapter.

## A Case Study

The author first served as minister of education at First Baptist Church, Saint Joseph, Missouri. Arriving in mid-April, 1948, his first task was to organize for Vacation Bible School (to be held the first week in June). High priority was enlisting the faculty. The most logical recourse seemed to personally enlist each worker.

Along came July and it was time to think about the Sunday School leadership for the fall. What was more natural than to enlist the workers personally, as he did for VBS. (He didn't even know he was in the trap!) By October, all positions were filled, but he was drained. In addition, many other tasks were left undone.

Finally, being uncomfortable in the trap, he decided to find another way. It came with the move to a new field in 1960. Recognizing the need for a better way, he delegated much of his authority to a church-elected nominating committee. The process worked like this:

1. The committee was authorized to make nominations to the church for all officers and leaders of the church, except church staff. *Delegation.*

2. The nominating committee was divided into subgroups for each church organization, with power to recommend to the nominating committee. *Delegation.*

3. The subcommittees visited in the home of each potential department director to discuss the importance of the position and ask for permission to place his/her name in nomination. *Delegation.*

4. After election of the department director by the church,

the subcommittee worked with the director in selecting the rest of the leadership in the department. *Delegation.*

5. The department director was authorized to enlist the persons approved by the committee. *Delegation.*

6. If mutually acceptable, these names were presented to the church for election. *Delegation.*

7. The department director was authorized to personally enlist a chorister and pianist. *Delegation.*

8. This process began in February of each year and continued through December, nominating deacons, treasurers, clerks, as well as all church organizational leadership.

By 1971, the church had grown to 4,400 members and over 600 church-elected leaders. All of these were personally counseled in their homes and evaluated by the nominating committee prior to their nomination and election. It was fortunate for the church that the minister of education found his way out of the delegation trap several years before. Even more fortunate was the staff man himself. By this time he would have been ready for the crazy box. Delegation wins again!

# 6

# Time Management

"I don't have the time!"

*Time Management is the maximum utilization of time in order to achieve your objective most effectively.*

## A Case Study

It was too good to be true. A local church in Atlanta had asked me to lead in their annual Bible study week. Fortunately, it was the book of Acts, with the emphasis on the beginnings of the missionary movement of the church. It lent itself to challenging the local church to follow the example of the Antioch church and the missionary zeal of the apostle Paul.

The pastor and minister of education had encouraged me to demonstrate creative ways of teaching. This was an important by-product, since many of those attending would be Sunday School teachers. I had just finished writing a thirteen-week series for adult Bible study in Acts and had oraganized it along the same lines as requested by the church.

The class could be taught two hours each week night, enabling me to give full time to my regular vocational work. To top it all off, they offered a most generous honorarium, considerably more than I had ever received before for any kind of extra ministry. It was a far cry from the early days of gasoline money and a set of cuff links!

Strange things emerge from such idyllic surroundings. The

clerk of the federal court sent me a summons for jury duty that same week. Little did I know that several crucial matters were going to surface regarding my regular work. They demanded immediate attention, and that meant going into the office very early each morning. The idyllic arrangement degenerated toward the predicament of the classic one-armed paperhanger. Leaving the house at 6:00 A.M. and returning at 10:00 P.M. meant that somebody, somewhere, was going to be shortchanged. (I just do not have sixteen hours of productive and creative energy.) Would it be my regular work? The jury scene? The church at Bible study?

As it turned out I tried to give my best efforts to the nightly Bible study. I might be able to take up the slack at my regular job and the other jurors might pull my weight for me. Surely, the Lord would see me through this bit of overscheduling. After all, was not I serving him by teaching his Word and serving in the cause of his justice?

The week began with excitement of the challenge. Each day took its drain and showed the strain. My wife gave her usual support, which was always more than I deserved and more than any man could ask.

The last straw came Thursday night. I dragged myself from the automobile into the house, gave a lip service greeting to my wife, sipped her offered cup of tea, and stared into space. She spoke. I stared. The following dialogue is verbatim. I shall never forget it.

"Bob, I just want to ask you one question."

"Yes?"

"What are you trying to prove?"

A long pause ensued, filled with my quizzical glance.

"What do you mean, 'What am I trying to prove?' "

"Well, you must be trying to prove something. No one can go at this pace without trying to prove something. Is it that you do not feel that you earn enough money to support our family?"

"No."

"Is it that you feel that the Bible will not be taught unless you teach it to the crosstown church?"

"No."

"Is it that you think you are invaluable to the kingdom?"

"No."

"Well, I ask you again. What are you trying to prove?"

Another long pause produced the confession. "I don't know. I want to do so many things that I try to do too many. *I just don't have the time.*"

At this point I had only confessed. Little did I know that I was on the road to a far-reaching commitment. It came right after she responded, "Your efforts to serve the kingdom are commendable. In the process you seem to have no time for your family or for your own spiritual growth."

It was as close to a Damascus Road experience as I ever had. In a moment, in a flash of insight, I saw the wisdom of the question and her evaluation. It did not require the usual hassle of charges and counter-charges. There was no need to be defensive. She had lovingly stated her diagnosis of a long, chronic, problem. I was not "prioritizing" my time in terms of my objective. My excuse was classic: "I don't have the time." Within ten seconds I volunteered a commitment to a new priority for the use of my time. I had as much time as anyone else.

## Locating the Traps

**Major Trap**—*There is a time shortage. Not enough hours, days, months, years. I want to get so much done that it is impossible to do it in the time available. Other people may have time to plan, take a full vacation, be with their family,* *enjoy leisure, read novels, write a book, and the like. But not me. I give every bit of my time doing the essentials. That doesn't leave any time for the extras.*

Any of us could have written the above paragraph. Is there a mortal who has not said, "There are not enough hours in the day?" That seems to be the only question when the real and probing question is, "How can I use the hours available to their best advantage?"

It is just another form of escapism to claim that others seem to have more time. Indeed, often it appears that way. What we do not know is the demands of their time.

Stop a minute and think of the persons who seem to get more done than the rank and file. How do they do it? We will stay in the trap if we try to excuse our poor use of time. That process may make the trap more tolerable, but it will not extricate us from the trap. Here are some common excuses:

1. Their job is not as responsible as mine.
2. I don't have enough staff.
3. My secretary isn't efficient.
4. You can't imagine my family responsibilities.
5. My health won't tolerate the pace.
6. My office environment won't allow concentration.
7. I could never catch up on my regular job, not to mention taking on any extravocational work.
8. It takes time to become involved with the personal needs of people.

Add your own pet excuses to these standard ones. Assuming we are well-motivated, we tend to find an excuse for our failure to achieve. A good excuse is more palatable than a poor one. But a poor one is better than no excuse. A realistic appraisal might be that other people seem to have more talents or gifts in using the available time. (But who wants to be that objective and admit it?) If the truth were known, the other "gifted" person may have disciplined himself over the years to become the master of time, rather than vice versa.

**Other Traps**—*1. I practice the "Open-Door Policy." My office is open to anyone at any time. If you are going to be a leader, you must be available. It may take a lot of time, but it is worth it.* An attractive trap, isn't it? In order to avoid the charge of having a closed door, we tend to overdo our availability to everyone. If we push the open-door concept too far, we eventually will face some other problems. (A) We spend so much time giving ourselves and listening to others that we have no time for filling up our emotional and spiritual reservoirs. (B) We have a life-style that is impossible to discipline. (C) We tend to force our family or secretaries to cover up for us and reply that we are not available. None of these seem to help in solving the problem.

But, are there no options to the two extremes? Of course there are: announced times for public availability, agreeing to see the person later in the day or week; talking briefly on the telephone.

*2. There are so many meetings that I must plan (or attend). You cannot imagine how much time they take. I meet myself coming and going. I told my associates the other day, "We've got to quit meeting like this!"* If you don't find yourself attending an abundance of meetings, then what do you do with all your time? Every manager is engaged in calling meetings. Therefore, the question is not whether to have meetings. The question is how to make your meetings advantageous, rather than a drain on your emotional, physical, and time-conscious being.

*3. If I could just get away from the telephone. People disrupt my concentration. They talk for hours on end. They call at the office, at my home, while I'm on vacation. If I could disconnect Mr. Bell's invention, I could save several hours a day.* On second thought, recognize some of the advantages of telephone communication when we want to get *our* message to others. It is possible to rig your instrument to operate on outgoing calls only. But that is as negative as the closed-door policy. The answer seems to lie in more efficient use of the telephone to your advantage, to meet your objective.

*4. Answering my correspondence takes so much time, you wouldn't believe it. I spend so much time with dictating equipment that I don't get to spend enough time with people.* Could it be that we do not know how to utilize this part of our daily work? Are we spending too much time in making a business letter into a literary masterpiece? Are we taking two pages to write what two paragraphs could do more effectively? Are we generating some correspondence that could better go undone? Are we using time-honored methods of the 1940s when we have easy access to the updated word processing procedures of today?

*5. Personal visits would take every hour of my day if I would let them. As it is, I seldom have time for my family because of the hours I spend talking with other people—home visitation, counseling, drop-in visitors, salesmen, and the like. And my ministry depends on contact with persons. I just don't have time left. What can I do?* Your solo voicing of this dilemma joins hundreds of others and becomes a giant chorus. Do not think you are alone in this problem. As in correspondence and telephone discipline, could it be that you are not managing well what time you do have? How vividly I remember one evening going to visit a prospect for our church with a deacon who knew the family from another city. Upon arriving at the home, they had one great reunion, talking about everything from their former church to Little League football. They agreed to visit our church (and later became excellent members). A good use of our time? Maybe? I neglected to tell you the visit took three and one-half hours! That is a total of seven man-hours. Could it be that we could have achieved the same objective in half that time and visited another family that same night?

6. *Who has time to take a day off? I can't even find time for a vacation. When you work seventy or so hours a week, how can you take a day off? The demands of this job do not even let me find time for that personal touch that I want to give to my associates*

Busy man, you have had a little day! Research upon research has shown that occasional time off is productive in the long run, be it coffee break, afternoon off, day off, or the scheduled vacation. It is only in this century that business and manufacturing personnel have enjoyed any holidays other than Christmas Day. And yet, today's worker can be a productive worker, when motivated.

It is not working that wears us out as much as pretending to work. I recall when working as a market analyst for Black, Sivalls, and Bryson, that some days there was not enough work to do in our office. I felt it necessary to pretend that I was busy. It seemed that 5:00 P.M. would never come. I was absolutely exhausted when I got home. The "busy" person does not necessarily get the job done. The organized person usually gets more done.

Good advice: Work smarter, not longer.

And about the personal touch. You either have it, or you don't. It is not something at which you must work. Your associates can tell. People are smarter than dogs. Dogs can instinctively tell whether you like them or not. It just can't be explained. The more serious trap is do you feel too important to be bothered. That really is bad news.

7. *I don't understand it. I use all of the time-savers written*

*in current articles. I have streamlined my office procedures, enabling me to minister outside of the office. And yet, I don't have enough time and the result is an unproductive ministry.*

This trap seems to be contradictive to the others. You have found some shortcuts and designed efficiency into your management style. But still little time is available and no results are attainable. But whoever said that shortcuts and efficiency makes for results? Maybe you have cut down and cut down until you have cut out the heart and spirit of your ministry. Some ministers mechanically visit every day every member who is hospitalized. But the visit is cold, quick, and self-defeating. Would it be better management of his time to visit every other day and stay longer at each visit? Or would a visit every third day (in noncrisis situations) allow him to make some other visits in the community that otherwise would go unheeded?

## Questionnaire

| Yes | No | |
|-----|-----|-----|
| ____ | ____ | 1. Is my time more important than my money? |
| ____ | ____ | 2. Is a calendar my only time support document? |
| ____ | ____ | 3. Do I plan my schedule longer than a month in advance? |
| ____ | ____ | 4. Am I willing to change a prearranged schedule? |
| ____ | ____ | 5. Do I usually get done what I plan to do? |
| ____ | ____ | 6. Do my associates feel that I have time for them? |
| ____ | ____ | 7. Do I feel bogged down in paperwork? |
| ____ | ____ | 8. Do incoming telephone calls hinder my work? |

_____ _____  9. Am I taking time to do things that could be delegated to others?

_____ _____  10. Am I oversupervising my associates?

_____ _____  11. Am I spending too much time doing and not enough time managing?

_____ _____  12. Does my open-door policy work to my advantage?

_____ _____  13. Do other people seem to have more time than I?

_____ _____  14. Do I plan my meetings to be time-savers rather than time-spenders?

_____ _____  15. Do I handwrite my letters?

_____ _____  16. Do I take my allotted vacation?

_____ _____  17. Do I tend to procrastinate and then forget?

_____ _____  18. Do I attempt too much at one time?

_____ _____  19. Do some snap decisions come back to hurt me?

_____ _____  20. Do I prefer to manage by the priorities of others?

_____ _____  21. Is the coffee break a time-waster, as a rule?

_____ _____  22. I don't have time to get my job done.

## How to Avoid the Time Traps

**General Guidelines**—There are so many traps in this area that it is risky to identify such a few. Since time is common to everyone in identical measure, time management becomes universal. Executive, laborer, homemaker, professor, student—everyone struggles with time management. Then why is it that so many never understand the solution to the riddle? Where does the time go? How time flies? Time is against us. There are not enough days in the week.

Oversimplified, the following time acrostic may help to get the answer to the riddle of time shortage.

P lanning your time in terms of your objective.

O rganizing to provide leisure and vocational time.

W orking consistently at your objective.

E valuating results in terms of time spent.

R eprioritizing your time for more effectiveness.

You will note some basic administrative overtones to the acrostic. Time management is basically the same as any other type of management. The power that good time management generates is not power over other people. It is to power yourself to accomplish what you set out to do in the same 168 hours per week available to everyone. Here are some general guidelines to assist.

*1. Nearly everyone wastes two hours every day.* That comes to thirty days a year. So all those things that executives say they don't have time for, they do have time for. That's what Merrill E. Douglass, director of the Time Management Center and author of the book *How to Control the Time of Your Life,* told participants at AMA's meeting on "Time Management," held in San Francisco, July 6–7, 1977.

In addressing the meeting, Douglass listed what he considers to be the biggest time wasters. *Interruptions, drop-in visitors, and telephone calls,* he said, constitute the greatest offenders. The second largest time wasters, in his opinion are being involved in too much detail and attempting to do too much at the same time. Then come crises: lack of objectives, deadlines, or priorities; meetings; and paperwork.

What can people do to schedule their work time better? In Douglass's opinion, the first thing that managers should do is clarify their objective and priorities. Decide on the best use of their time.

*2. To the administrator who says that he "ran out of time,"*

*James L. Hayes, president of AMA says, "Actually, no one can 'run out of time.' "* [1] Time is a rentless commodity hour after hour, day after day, week after week. Unlike money, it must be spent; like money, it may be wisely spent or squandered.

So what appears to be a problem with the availability of time is really a problem of misspent time. Like the hapless do-it-yourselfer who paints himself into a corner, the manager, who suddenly finds that there's no time to do something critical, hasn't been paying enough attention to what he or she has been doing.

The real value of managerial time expenditure depends on both the amount of energy invested and the appropriateness of activities undertaken. By doubling your energy, for example, you can get twice as much done in a given period thus, in effect, doubling its value. But if the activity involved is irrelevant to the job or is something that someone else should have done, you have wasted your managerial energy and devalued the time you spent.

Hayes further says that the basics in time management involve (1) Taking a personal time inventory to find out where the workday actually goes. (2) Planning activities in order of priority to ensure that first things do come first, instead of being inadvertently preempted by the trivial. (3) Delegating properly to free managerial time for managerial activities.

*3. Most every speaker on time management lists time thieves.* Most lists will include these, by one name or the other. (Not necessarily in order of thievery.)

| | |
|---|---|
| Unproductive meetings | Crisis decisions |
| Attempting too much at once | Can't say no |
| | Can't say yes |
| Failing to delegate | Lack of authority |
| Needless telephone calls | Poor planning |

| | |
|---|---|
| Inadequate information | Snap decisions |
| Goals too high | Making same mistake twice |
| Goals too low | Lack of good policies |
| Outside demands | Flood of correspondence |
| Television | Doing instead of managing |
| Lack of priorities | Lack of self-discipline |
| Procrastination | Unavailability of the boss |
| Uncertain objectives | Job expectancy not clear |
| Office interruptions | Fatigue |
| Undue socializing | |

As you look at the list, note that some of our favorite time stealers are conspicuous by their absence. For instance, nonproductive associates, inefficient secretaries, poor working conditions, unreasonable boss, unrealistic responsibilities, impossible task, job lacks potential. These are usually the excuses we give. They major on passing the buck and sharing the blame with someone else. When we take time to be objective, most of our time stealers originate with ourselves. Pogo was right when he declared, "We have met the enemy and he is us."

*4. A group of doctoral students at Midwestern Theological Seminary provided the following lists.* All of them had been out of the seminary five years or more and made their observations from their experiences in local fields.

### Effective Use of My Time
### (Listed in order of effectiveness)

1. Quiet time with God
2. Family togetherness
3. Setting objectives and priorities
4. Counseling
5. Preparation for preaching/teaching
6. Training others

7. Leisure
8. Community involvement
9. Continuous education

### Ineffective Use of My Time
### (Listed in Order of ineffectiveness)

1. Failing to delegate
2. Procrastination
3. Poor planning
4. Failing to make a daily schedule
5. Failing to "prioritize"
6. Open-door policy
7. Telephone
8. Ineffective meetings
9. Television
10. Failing to evaluate

*5. A fundamental barrier in time utilization is failing to understand the difference between* urgent *and* important. Given some thinking time, you can probably state the difference between the two. But ask yourself this question, Do I make my daily decisions for time utilization based upon my academic knowledge of these two words?

*Urgent* has an immediacy about it. The job must be done now, or it cannot be done at all. It may not be very important. Assume that your decision is between watching an 8:00 P.M. television program or reading this book. If it is 7:59 P.M., that is urgent. Probably not important. You may be able to see the television program on its rerun, and you can read the book tomorrow.

*Important* has a crucial consequence about it. The job must eventually be done or the entire objective will suffer. It may not be urgent. Assume that your decision is being attending to pastors' conference at noon or working on the proposed long-range plan for the church. You can attend the luncheon meeting if you wish, since the deadline for your recommendation to the church council is two months off. However, if you consistently put off the important matters in preference to urgent matters, you will soon have a real crisis on your hands. That is, you have to make a time decision that involves two matters that are both urgent and important. Usually, this is caused by failing to handle important tasks before the deadline arrives.

**Specific Guidelines**—*1. Reduce your objectives to writing and keep them in front of your planning processes.* A card on your desk or a note in your date book will serve as a discipline when you want to decide how to use your time. Take some time to establish your priorities in terms of your objective and specific deadlines. You may want to do this monthly. Thirty minutes spent in this way may save hours and maybe days during the next month. You made your decision some time ago, and now all you have to do is carry it out. Naturally, emergencies may change your direction. This in known as "managing by exception" and is a faithful friend to the effective administrator.

At the end of the month look at your calendar to see how well you stayed by your priorities. Learn from your own mistakes and affirm your discipline by your success. At the same time, determine your priorities for the next month.

*2. Use your desk calendar as your master calendar.* Transfer each week's schedule to a pocket-sized card that will stick to you closer than a brother for that week. You can make penciled changes on it throughout the week if needed.

This keeps your immediate information where you need it, in your pocket. It keeps long-range dates where they are most functional and the safest, on your desk. If you have a secretary, trust and train her to make office appointments for you. This makes you available to your associates. She may make a few mistakes in underbooking or overbooking appointments at first. But she will learn. The safety factor lies in the situation of not being trapped into takng an engagement just because you do not have another appointment.

How many leaders have accepted engagements only because the inquirer asked if that date were available. The unsuspecting administrator whips out the traditional annual pocket calendar and is trapped. His inquirer knows that the date is available. What can you do? Be candid and say, "No, I don't want to come." Far better to ask the person to write you a note and check it with your desk calendar when you get back to the office. In the meantime you can decide whether that meeting is supportive of your objectives or of his objectives only. In some cases, you will need to be candid and tell the inquirer that the date is not filled with another engagement but that you need that time for other matters.

Almost universally successful salespeople spend the last few minutes of the working day reevaluating how they intend to spend the hours of the next day. They say those few minutes are the most productive time of the day. Maybe religious leaders could take a note from their notebook. Let's don't take their practicality and "baptize" it by equating it with our evening devotional time. They are both important, but different processes.

3. *The telephone can be another Dr. Jekyll and Mr. Hyde.* What would we ever do without it? Books have been written about its two-faced character. Let's see if we can capsule the essence of its capabilities to steal time from us. (But let's not be fooled: No inanimate object can steal anything from us. We lose it by default!)

Most of the time the telephone aids us when we want to talk to someone else. It tends to rob us of time when others want information from us. Therefore, take care about the time spent on incoming calls. (This is not to be selfish. If your objective is not selfish, then your priorities will probably not be selfish.) By your placing the call, our culture's courtesy allows you to initiate its termination. The alternative has kept many of us on the line for hours.

It is recognized that this principle cuts across the grain for some people. Let us use the long-distance call as an example. The telephone company has done an unbelievable job of making us think a long-distance call is both urgent and important. When someone announces that we have a call from another city, what do we usually do? Drop everything (and everybody) and rush to the phone. But wait a minute. What does that say to the person with whom you are talking? What if it comes during a private prayer in your office? How many times have you received a long-distance call from someone who wanted to give you something? Do they not usually want something from you? Then should it not fit into your priority system?

Perhaps this seems a bit cold to you. It need not, for the essence of your being will be interpreted after you get on the line. Many of us in religious work are so sensitive about the feelings of others that we lose sight of our objective. We can be "thrifty, brave, clean, and reverent" until we become Eagle Scouts and fail to accomplish our goals. Still seems cold? Recall when Jesus' mother came to ask him to help out with the impending social crisis of the Cana wedding? At first, he balked because it did not aid in the accomplishment of his objective. Later, he performed the miracle to use as a foundation sign for his ministry.

*4. Correspondence can generally be cut in half by cutting our letters in half.* Victorian rhetoric and business clichés are out-of-date. A good letter has four parts. State the purpose of the letter. Explain the details as needed. Be specific in what response you want the reader to make. Add any personal note that you think appropriate and productive. Often this latter feature is done with a "P.S." which is now the most read portion of the average letter.

We misjudge our readership when we assume that they value our appreciation of them in direct proportion to the length of our correspondence. The exact opposite is generally the case. Busy persons respond better to brief, direct mail.

Most executives find it helpful to handle their correspondence the first thing in the morning. It not only allows their secretaries to finalize it before the afternoon mail goes out but also relieves the mental anxiety of needing to get to that task throughout the day.

Time studies have shown the most expensive ways to originate a letter are in this order: handwrite the letter and have it typed; let the stenographer take it in shorthand and transcribe it; put your message on dictating equipment at your leisure and have it transcribed at the leisure of the stenographer. If you are an organization with as many as five persons initiating correspondence, you should look into more sophisticated systems of word processing.

Since the cost of sending the average business letter has now reached over five dollars a letter, we should be careful of the way we use this communication device for both the economy of time and money.

*5. Drop-in visits to your office seem to have a double or nothing consequence to them.* Both helpful and distracting. You can neither close the door forever nor can you continually have the open door. A closed door with a sign on the doorknob saying, "Please interrupt," may be a good compromise.

Give your secretary specific instructions concerning how

to treat visitors and incoming phone calls. Most callers understand the need for occasional privacy or conferences. When
visitors come without an appointment, they should expect some
delay or that you might not be in the office that day. Your
secretary can then make a specific appointment for them at
a later date.

Once your guest is in the office, his mission will determine
how long you can comfortably talk with him (as compared to
what you had planned to do with that time.) Your seat placement and body language will give him some hint as to your
availability. Sitting across the desk indicates formality and
strictly business. Using straight chairs is emblematic of brevity.
Overstuffed furniture is an invitation for informal, casual, and
unhurried conversation. When you put your feet on the table,
your guest knows that you have plenty of time. When you
sit on the edge of your chair, he knows your time is limited
and so is his.

Interoffice conversation is tricky at this point. Some managers think it is a status symbol to have associates come to their
office. Maybe it is. It is also a potential time-waster. An American business proverb could be, "He that goes into another's
office has the advantage of choosing when to leave." Obviously,
there are exceptions. Do you want to use your time effectively?
It is up to you. The hourglass grins as it prophesies: "Pay me
now, or pay me later."

*6. Meetings. Meetings. Meetings.* There are those that are
effective, ineffective, and those that the boss calls, and who
is to say. But like so many other time traps, they can be helpful.
You are the one to decide, especially if you are the supervisor.
Try these suggestions for better meetings.

1. Write down the purpose of the meeting and expected
   results.

2. Determine who would profit the meeting with their attendance.

3. Establish a proposed agenda. Share it in advance with those who will be invited for their input and preparation.

4. Have your secretary verify that contributing members will be available at the time set. Change time, if possible, to get full participation.

5. Start on time.

6. Accept all input and have it recorded by someone other than yourself. You cannot moderate and take minutes at the same time.

7. Ask, and expect, divergent opinions. Why else did you need a meeting? Determine the intensity of the divergency.

8. Look for alternatives.

9. Give full explanation as necessary.

10. Have necessary research done in advance.

11. Review actions taken at the meeting prior to adjourning, noting assigned responsibility.

12. Note time of any future deadlines or meetings.

13. Adjourn on time.

Some of the best meetings are stand-up meetings. Some of the most productive are three-day retreats. A meeting's importance and urgency determines the length.

If the meeting was called to find group consensus, then keep moving until you feel you have it. If its purpose was for information for your ultimate decision, let that be known at the outset. Remember a management decision long delayed is one cause of a morale problem.

When evaluating your meeting (always an important aspect of managing), consider what can be accomplished in

seventy minutes. President Carter asked several denominational executives for lunch at the White House. He hosted the
meal, engaged in proper interpersonal conversation, proposed
a massive volunteer missionary movement among Southern
Baptists, received enthusiastic support of the autonomously related agencies, and told everyone good-bye, all in seventy
minutes.

7. *Cluttered desks may give the appearance of being overworked. More than likely they indicate underorganization.* An
immaculately clean desk can be just as deceiving. Anyone can
stuff the papers into empty drawers and closets five minutes
before your arrival. Consider these practical suggestions.

• Use the traditional "incoming" and "outgoing" boxes. Be
sure you at least look at all material in the incoming box prior
to leaving for the day. Ask your secretary to remove all material
from the outgoing box in time for the afternoon mail. Make
a notation on anything that needs urgent handling.

• Reserve certain portions of your desk for papers that fall
into the following classifications: (A) Letters to be answered.
(B) Matters to be discussed with persons in the organization.
(C) Matters that you must handle that day and those that can
be handled later. (D) Material that you want to read sometime
in the future.

• Use your wastebasket frequently. If in doubt, put the
matter in the pile to be looked at later; it usually will be delayed
one day getting to the round file.

Try to handle most paperwork only once. It takes time
to read and get the essence of the material. A second handling
wastes time. When in doubt, make a penciled note concerning
the decision to be made later.

Keep memos as infrequent and brief as possible. But they
are an indispensible interoffice communication time-saver.

They help you get the message on paper when it is convenient to you and allows the reader to read it at his convenience. Take caution to avoid using memos to avoid face-to-face conversation. Alienation is sure to follow.

## A Case Study

Jack Lawson had completed his seminary training and had profitably pursued a year's graduate training in pastoral and interpersonal relationships. He was well-liked by his peers and he liked other persons. He was one of those unusual people who genuinely likes everyone.

Upon accepting the leadership of his second church, he felt that his objective would be helping that church grow spiritually and physically. A second objective was the establishing of a mission church in a contiguous community.

Jack began by gaining church and community-at-large acceptance. He was visible in public places, attended civic meetings, and supported community projects. Similarly, he regularly visited the sick, the bereaved, the depressed, the unsaved, the unenlisted, you name them, and he had ministered to their needs.

The church showed an immediate response to such care and concern. After a year or so, the church's growth seemed to plateau. Jack redoubled his time for people. Always available to talk with people at their convenience and for the duration of their pleasure. No doubt about it, Jack was a popular pastor and community personality.

After another year, the plateau was still laid out on a straight line. When he reassessed his objectives, it became apparent that some adjustments were needed. Jack and his family took a few days off his regular work schedule. His rationale was that he was not getting the job done working seventy hours a week, so what would a few days in planning matter?

If you are not succeeding in goal achievement, it is only a matter of the degree of your failure. Why not risk a few days for reflection and planning?

With time at an abundance and distractions at a minimum, he began to reflect on his ministry of three years. Acceptance? Yes! Objective reached? No! Failure as a minister? No! Reappraisal of objective? Confirmed! Then what changes in his use of time should be made? Heretofore, there was no time to plan with the deacons and church school leadership regarding church growth. While he engaged in an abundance of personal visitation, he did not take the lead in a churchwide program of enlistment. When he tried to be factual in determining how he utilized his time week-by-week, he found he did not have the information. The minivacation ended with the decision to make a time study of his activities over a period of two months.

The results validated his suspicions. He was not using his time to accomplish what he had set out to do. What could he do to get back on the track? He listed everything he thought he needed to do each week and the amount of time normally taken for that activity. It totaled 125 hours.

Obviously, some priority needed to be set to reduce the activities to some reasonable time frame. He reassessed the time he would allow for certain actions based upon his objective. Hard decisions. Some of the things he enjoyed doing most were drastically reduced. Some eliminated.

His calendar was reordered appropriately.

One year later he reevaluated his objectives, his time utilization, and his calendar for the next year. He was happier for he was attaining some portions of the objective he had sought. His family was happier for they were included in his priority schedule. The church was happier for they found more joy in the growth of the church than in their abundant interpersonal relations with the pastor.

# 7

# Success

*Success is the attainment of your objective as measured by your value system.*

## A Case Study

Old First Church had suffered a lack of growth and had attributed it to the leadership of the former pastor, now retired. In seeking a new pastor, they give him their expectations of growth, immediately, if not sooner.

Pastor Johnson wanted to set a spiritual basis for his ministry and felt that growth would come as a result of God's providence. The barriers to immediate growth were considerable and at the end of the first year, the pastor gave his estimate of the average worship attendance on Sunday morning to be 450. (Actually, it was only 372.) The Sunday School general director wanted his organization to show support and he counted the "hall-walkers' class" and other associated persons in the building, plus an estimate of how many probably were present, but not counted. These totaled 465. (But only 384 really were in classes each week.)

The leadership proudly called attention to the "significant growth of our church during the last year." The membership was pleased at the announcement. Reverend Johnson had some pinches of his conscience, since he felt pretty sure that there was not much growth, if any. Yet, pressured by the church's expectations, he let the people enjoy their moment of success for a season.

The following year did not hold much more promise or statistical increase. Johnson began to press his leadership for more attendance. The staff was told in no uncertain terms that they must record thirty visits each week. Sunday School departments were assigned goals by the general director. The pastor did not expect others to do what he was unwilling to do, and he tried to make at least forty prospect visits each week. Because of many other responsibilities, the pastor and staff made their visits brief, somewhat impersonal, and occasional by counterproductive.

The Sunday School staff got the message and redoubled their efforts to raise the average attendance. Spending considerable time in prospect and absentee visitation, they had to let something go undone. That happened to be their formerly well-prepared lessons and fellowship cultivation of the regular attenders.

Lo and behold, at the end of the year, the average worship attendance as guesstimated by the pastor was 500 (actually, only 395.) The Sunday School reported 545, by their own methods. Note, there was some real growth, in adddition to the statistical wishful thinking.

Several years have now passed. There is no rebellion, but no enthusiasm either. Perhaps the attitude would best be described as the Laodecean blahs. Into that vacuum marched some inquisitive minds wondering what was missing in their church life. The inevitable happened: a committee was appointed. Here is what they discovered.

1. The actual count of morning worshipers that year averaged 372. The pressure on the pastor for member increase had shown up in his lack of sermon preparation.

2. The Sunday School averaged only 365. The peak year was 435, but attendance began to drop when members attending were becoming bored with poor content and methods of learning. Then, too, the general secretary counted only those who were actually in class.

3. The deacons were noticing a lack in their spirit, as was the staff and other church leadership. Evidently, the pressure for numbers and too many half-hearted visits had sapped their spirit. And where was that former general secretary that had inflated the figures?

4. The pastor was depressed. He wondered just what had pushed him from his pastoral life-style to be driven to show a Madison Avenue life-style. The staff felt their calling had been derailed into a promotional rut.

Each person of the committee capsuled their opinion. Jake said, "He who lives by statistics will die by statistics." Jane commented, "It matters not whether you win or lose, but how you play the game." Ed countered with, "It matters not how you play the game, but whether you win or lose." Dan summed up the matter when he facetiously stated, "Only the bottom line counts."

## Locating the Traps

**Major Trap**—*Only the bottom line counts. Everything else is secondary. You can say what you want, the church is expecting growth, big growth. By that they mean numerical and financial growth. Don't worry about such things as spiritual growth and maturity or about caring for needs of persons. Just keep those cards and letters and members and dollars coming.*

If you think this trap has been overdrawn, overexposed, and overextended, you may be underinformed. It only looks so crass because several years of life of a church have been capsuled into a few sentences.

Where did we get such ideas and models? Straight from our television sets via Madison Avenue. Straight from the business world via Wall Street. Straight from government via city hall. The advertisers have convinced us that "more is better." Corporate presidents have taught us that the only concern of our organization is "the amount of profit." The mayor agrees with the chamber of commerce "that we must grow at any cost." Altogether, they have convinced us that we must accede to the standards of others even if we lose our souls in the process.

Perhaps the most poignant illustration can be drawn from the recent best-seller, *All the President's Men*.[1] It does not compare one political party's ethics against another as much as it compares human standards against God's standards. One scene takes place in the newsroom of the *Washington Post*. James Dooley, former head of the Committee to Reelect the President, has just come in and said he needed to talk to someone.

He told reporter Woodward that CRP had rigged station WTTG's poll on whether the people supported the president's decision about the Haiphong mining. The media had asked people to send in cards indicating whether they agreed or disagreed with the president on the mining. Sample ballots were placed in advertisements in the *Post* and the *Star*.

Dooley said that the CRP press office ran the rigging. Everyone employed was expected to fill out fifteen postcards. Ten people worked for days buying different kinds of stamps and cards and getting different handwriting to fake the responses. Thousands of newspapers were bought from the newsstands and the ballots were clipped out and mailed in.

Dooley indicated that at least 4,000 ballots supporting Nixon's decision were sent from CRP. The television station reported that 5,157 agreed with the president and 1,158 disagreed. Had the CRP ballots not been sent in, the president would, at best, have lost by one vote—1,158 to 1,157.

Woodward called a CRP spokesman and asked if the poll had not been rigged. "When you're involved in an election, you do what you can," the man replied. "We assumed the other side [McGovern forces] would do it also. On that assumption, we proceeded. I don't know if the other side did."

Following it down to the end, Woodward called McGovern's former campaign aide. "We didn't do it," he said somewhat incredulously. "It didn't occur to us, believe me. These guys are something. They assume we have the same sleazy ethics as theirs."

A recent quote from the world of athletics brings the price of success into focus for the believer. Conrad Dobler is an all-pro offensive lineman formerly with the Saint Louis Cardinals' football team. He had gained the reputation of the dirtiest lineman in the league. Such a reputation seems to have served his advantage in publicity and intimidation of the opposition. In an article in Eastern Airline's *Review* (November 1977), his mother is quoted as being unconcerned about his image, saying, "If that helps bring in money to the stadium, well . . ." Linda Dobler, Conrad's wife, occasionally worried about the effect Conrad's reputation would have on their son, Mark, but the boy seemed to be able to differentiate between Number 66 on the field and the person who was his father. Once when Mark was being taunted by a schoolmate about his father's play, Mark ended the discussion by saying, "He's only doing his job."

That seems to be a heavy price to pay for success.

The age-old philosophy of, "The end justifies the means"

might have some merit, if the "end" were what God would have us do. Yet, is it possible that God would have us do anything to achieve his ends if our means were less than righteous?

Look at the other side of that argument. The means are not the end. You can do many things well and noble and still not achieve your end (objective). This is the old problem of managing by activities and not by objectives.

You can twist these words in any shape you want to, but it seems that God is going to expect performance in both "means" and "ends." Actually, "only the bottom line counts" is the only real measurement for the Christian church or leader *if* (and that is the biggest two-letter word in administrative rationale) God determines what makes up the bottom line and if Christian leaders seek the Spirit of Christ in trying to achieve a "successful" bottom line.

Sometimes Christians use the phrase, "Beyond the bottom line." They explain that their immediate objective could be attained *plus* a closer relationship to God in the process. Often we think of corporations as being coldhearted, interested only in the dollar. Yet, in a recent financial page of the *Atlanta Constitution* was this concept. The lead article's headline read, "Corporations are interested in more than profit and loss." It went on to say that profit only aids a business to do other things.

**Minor Traps**—There are so many of these, they are called Legion. Only seven are listed here, with a biblical illustration. Every case cited is a person who probably thought he was doing the proper thing, something approved by his peer group, and condoned by the culture. He had molded his life-style around his value system and ultimately he fell into the trap of false success. Do you recognize these traps?

*1. Materialism.* Look at the rich young ruler and the rich

farmer. They had set out to achieve things through wealth. They had arrived. What more could they want. (This is a great temptation today in our affluent society.)

2. *Fame.* Remember Herod Antipas? He had notoriety and was ruler over Galilee for over thirty years. Everyone knew his name, and most people trembled at the mention of it. Yet, when he came face-to-face with Jesus, our Lord would not even dignify Herod's questions with an answer. (What one of us has not wanted to see our names and pictures in the local or religious newspaper?)

3. *Power.* Consider Caiaphas. Even the Romans recognized the power of the high priest. Ultimately, he had the power to influence the sentencing of Jesus to the cross. (If monetary gain is not the aim of Christian leaders, oftentimes we succumb to the power syndrome.)

4. *Intellectualism.* Visualize Nicodemus, educated, bright, a lawyer, and a leading citizen of Jerusalem. He had reached the top: president of the chamber of commerce, director of the educational television station, WJEW, chairman of the United Way campaign. Yet, he knew that he had the wrong bottom line, the wrong concept of success. (In our search for knowledge, we may come to be educated fools.)

5. *Pseudospiritualism.* Behold the Pharisees. If you don't think they felt they were the alpha and omega of God's plan for his people, just ask them. No need for modesty—if you've got it, flaunt it. Yet, Jesus was most severe in his judgment against them. "Snakes—whitewashed sepulchers—hypocrites!" (Just observe those looking down their noses who seem to think they have a corner on the Truth.)

6. *Playing Games and Surviving.* Pilate is the epitome of this trap. He could play games with the Jews and the Romans, the rich and the poor, the religious and the vulgar, all at the same time. He just kept changing the ground rules or changing

audiences. If he could just be the winner of the current game, he thought he would be the champion of all. At least, he would survive in the hellhole of the Roman Empire. (What are those games we play? with our church? our denomination? our peers? our associates? our families? Worst off all, with ourselves? If we play these games, who is kidding whom that we are really surviving? surviving what?)

7. *Ladder Climbing.* See Saul: educated under Gamaliel; the rising star on the intellectual horizon of Judaism; zealous defender of the faith; persecutor of those heretical fanatics called "Christians." He practiced the dangerous game of getting ahead by stepping on others. He forgot the advice to be nice to others on the way up because you never know who you will need on the way down. (Is it possible that we confuse our ladder climbing with Jacob's ladder experience? When we get to the top of our "ladder," will we really be where we want to be?)

## Value Preference Chart

Rank the following according to your real reward system. (Give number one to the most important item.) As you consider the elements that make up your bottom line of success, be honest with yourself. God already knows how you feel. The value of this emotional exercise is to help you objectify your real goals in life.

_____ $30,000 worth of life insurance
_____ Supervising three persons
_____ Stylish clothing
_____ Own your home (debt free)
_____ Feeling fulfilled in your occupation
_____ Well-known author
_____ A "born again" believer

_____ Good health
_____ $30,000 annuity at age 65
_____ Abundance of food
_____ Happy family life
_____ Multitude of friends
_____ Fruitful witness

## How to Avoid the Success Trap

This may well be the hardest trap of them all to avoid. It is lodged somewhere between the will and the ego. Temptations are everywhere beckoning us to "come right this way." Among them are our bank account, peer approval, consumerism, self-satisfaction, status, survival need, security, and their first cousins. Like all other traps, one does not realize the danger until it is too late. Pogo's famous tactical quote seems to apply here, also. At least Pogo recognized the enemy. Sometimes that is our basic problem.

What is success? Take another look at the definition on the chapter title page. If that does not meet your concept of success, then write your own definition on that page. Maybe we can more easily characterize what success is not.

From the Christian perspective, success will differ from the world's value definition in terms of what is measured. In either case it is achieving your desired objective. By the world's value system, success is temporal, sensual, emotional, and physical. It is something that makes you feel good *now*.

Christianity has both a *here* and *hereafter* aspect to it. We judge our success by how it feels now and will feel later, and forever. How does it please me? my family? my community? most of all, my God? How will it appear in the world and in heaven?

Church people talk much about life hereafter, but they

act like there is only death hereafter. We quote Scripture about how this world's life is but a twinkling of an eye, but we live like it is the only life that counts. We have a theology of eternity but a "prac-tology" of threescore and ten. Our orthodoxy counsels people to lay up for themselves treasures in heaven, but our "orthopraxy" teaches to store everything we can in our barns, for tomorrow we die.

If we could just marry our Sunday concepts with our week-day precepts, we could avoid these traps. Or, we would know-ingly seek them out as our haven of security in this world. (The reason I am so familiar with the traps and these inconsistencies is that I have been there.)

### Biblical Guideposts

What does the Bible have to say about success? Jesus' entire life is a model for us. His first quotation in the Temple at age twelve indicates that he was aware of the difference between the world's standard and his standard. While his parents wanted him to conform to the pattern of all other Jewish boys, he knew that he must be about his Father's business.

More traditional models of Christ's concept of success show him washing the disciples feet, not desiring public acclaim, and the ultimate model of his atoning death for friend and foe alike. Since Jesus always practiced what he preached, we can rely upon his spoken word to teach us the true meaning of success. In researching these texts, many more were found, but these seven should provide us with ample cognitive reasons to see how Jesus differentiated his value system for those of his world and of ours.

"For who is more important, the one who sits at the table or the waiter? Is it not the one who sits at the table? But I am among you as one who serves" (Luke 22:27, Berkeley).[2]

"Unless your hearts are changed and become as little children, ye shall not enter into the kingdom of heaven" (Matt. 18:3, Rieu).[3]

"Whoever humbles himself like this child is greatest in the kingdom of heaven" (Matt. 18:4.)

"What shall a man give in exchange for his soul?" (Mark 8:37).

"But many that are first shall be last; and the last shall be first" (Matt. 19:30).

"Never blow your own horn in public, as the hypocrites are in the habit of doing on the street corners" (Matt. 6:2, Williams).[4] Jesus included this advice for praying, almsgiving, and fasting:

"For what shall it profit a man, if he shall gain the whole world, and lose his own soul?" (Mark 8:36).

If you wish a longer discourse on the characteristics of the kingdom citizen, read the entire Sermon on the Mount, Matthew 5—7. Measure these ideals against your ideas of success.

Three other biblical quotes are pertinent for this foundation. "Because thou sayest, I am rich, and increased with goods, and have need of nothing; and knowest not that thou art wretched, and miserable, and poor, and blind, and naked: I counsel thee to buy of me gold tried in the fire, that thou mayest be rich" (Rev. 3:17–18).

"For I was envious at the foolish, when I saw the prosperity of the wicked" (Ps. 73:3).

"Behold, these are the ungodly, who prosper in the world; they increase in riches" (Ps. 73:12).

Perhaps the most pointed of biblical warnings is Paul's: "The love of money is the root of all evil" (1 Tim. 6:10). Maybe we could paraphrase that and say that the love of money and egotism is the root of all pseudosuccess.

## Contemporary Landmarks

Aside from these basic biblical injunctions, there are a few contemporary helps. First, defeat can be a great education. Do you know anyone who has succeeded before the experience of some failure? Can you really say that you have learned how to do it right? (Your first attempt that succeeded may have been just plain luck. After you have failed, you will know for sure when you have at last succeeded.)

Second, "big shots" are usually little shots who kept on shooting. A friend of mine is the president of a large textile mill in the South. His Sunday School friends would tease him about how lucky he was in his business life. His comment seemed classic to me: "It's strange, but the harder I work the luckier I get."

Third, stopping at third base never adds to the score. You can do many things perfect, but if you do not follow through to your intended objective, it is mostly in vain, exercises in futility. Many a lover did everything right except to lead his intended bride to the altar of God to be his mate. The dating and engagement periods are only prelude to the wedding rites. Analyze your failures and see if some of them were caused by stopping at third base.

Fourth, William E. Holder said, "Success is good management in action." It seems that there is merit in translating this from the business world into the church and home environment. Apply the principles of this book into your everyday life, and see if you do not feel a sense of success that you did not enjoy before.

Fifth, Owen D. Young advised that we must be willing to pay the price.

There is a single reason why 99 out of 100 average businessmen never become leaders. That is their unwillingness to pay the price of responsibility. By the price of responsibility I mean hard driving, continual work . . . the courage to make decisions, to stand the gaff . . . the scourging honesty of never fooling yourself about yourself. You travel the road to leadership heavily laden. While the nine-to-five-o'clock worker takes his ease, you are "toiling upward through the night." Laboriously you extend your mental frontiers. Any new effort, the psychologists say, wears a new groove in the brain. And the grooves that lead to the heights are not made between nine and five. They are burned by midnight oil.[5]

Sixth, Rothchild gave seventeen rules for business success. While Rothchild was a noted businessman, he was not writing for a Christian theological journal when he outlined these rules for success.

"1. Carefully examine every detail of the business.
2. Be prompt.
3. Take time to consider and then decide quickly.
4. Dare to go forward.
5. Bear your trouble patiently.
6. Maintain your integrity as a sacred thing.
7. Never tell business lies.
8. Make no useless acquaintances.
9. Never try to appear something more than you are.
10. Pay your debts promptly.
11. Learn how to risk your money at the right time.
12. Shun strong liquor.
13. Employ your time well.
14. Do not reckon on chance.
15. Be polite to everyone.
16. Never be discouraged.
17. Work hard and you will succeed." [6]

Seventh, do not commit yourself at too dear a price for success, for it will either be too costly economically, emotionally, and spiritually, or will not produce a significant dividend.

Here are ways to improve your chances of success as a manager. Assuming that your value system is in good working order, these may be helpful in your daily administration of your work. These are edited from an article in *Advanced Management Journal.*

*1. Developing Self-Insight.* If you are truly interested in your own growth as a manager, you must begin by objectively as possible sizing up yourself in terms of personal strengths and limitations, your goals and developmental needs. Mere critical self-awareness is only the beginning of functional self-insight. With awareness of one's need for attitude or behavior modification must come the desire and will to change.

*2. Becoming People-Oriented.* The main job of a manager is to work for, with, and through others to achieve organizational goals. To effectively manage people, one must be aware of his impact upon them, and the real skill of the effective manager is that he is able to get others to accept his ideas and at the same time keep their own sense of participation, involvement, and accomplishment.

*3. Assuming, Rather than Merely Accepting, Responsibility.* The successful manager does not merely accept an assignment, fulfill it to the best of his ability, and then wait for another assignment. He is constantly and aggressively working to expand his role and influence in the organization. What enables him to be so effective is directly related to his attitude toward his job responsibility. He has developed that attitude that it is his obligation to relieve his superiors of as much of their workload as possible, not egotistically to expand his role at their expense but to free them for even bigger responsibilities.

*4. Becoming a Calculated Risk-Taker.* The successful manager realizes that he is expected by both superiors and subordinates to have the knowledge and experience required to make definite decisions and to see that they are implemented and executed. Calculated risk-taking is not gambling but is rather having the confidence that one has the ability, experience, knowledge, and acumen that will allow the organization to act and react so that its competitive position is protected and enhanced in the marketplace. The successful executive is well aware that calculated risk-taking is not intuition alone. He makes good use of the modern tools of administrative control exemplified by management information systems which provide on time, accurate data and intelligent information.

5. *Becoming Results-Oriented.* The results-oriented manager is constantly trying new ways to improve efficiency and productivity. He is not satisfied with the status quo; he is very receptive to new ideas, methods, procedures, systems, and techniques. However, unlike his less successful colleagues, he does not get bogged down in these means but keeps himself steadily oriented toward the end, cutting through the red tape that keeps him from realizing his objectives. He has no patience for bureaucratic paper shuffling; instead, he follows up and audits to see that the systems being used are producing results. If they are not, he finds innovative ways of overcoming the roadblocks.

6. *Developing Generalist as well as Specialist Skills.* The successful manager is constantly endeavoring to broaden himself beyond his technical specialty. He may do this through continuing his business education, learning new management methods and techniques. He may want to learn the functional responsibilities of his fellow managers, appreciating the interrelationships of departments. He can seek out and profit from constructive criticism and develop as much mutuality and rapport with fellow managers as possible without neglecting his own assigned responsibility.

7. *Identifying with Organizational Goals.* Identification

means considering one's self part of an integrated team whose members are working with mutual confidence toward common objectives. The complexity of modern business dictates the integrated team approach, but each member must pull his share of the load.

We would add a postscript for the Christian manager. His prayers should be generously with, "Teach me Thy ways, Lord;" "Give me wisdom, Lord;" and "nevertheless not my will, but Thy will be done."

## A Case Study

During my lifetime, I have had five pastors. Each has made a significant contribution to my spiritual growth, as well as having taught me some of the administrative truths shared in this book. My present pastor, William Self, is a communicator. J. T. Ford is a planner. Dotson Nelson is a decision-maker. Adiel Moncrief is an evaluator. The late Geoffrey Swadley, pastor during my high school and young adult years, taught me how to strive for success, as measured by my value system.

Pastor Swadley came to our conservative church in 1939. The congregation lived in a lower to middle economic neighborhood. Some of our more vocal members majored in hating, rather than loving. Others felt that God had given them the only "official" interpretation of his Word. My parents were somewhat uncomfortable in such a setting, but they persevered and insisted that I do likewise. It was not an exciting scene for a fourteen-year-old boy.

Enter Dr. Swadley, perhaps my most unforgettable character. He was then approaching forty, with a wide grin, a Midwestern mountain twang, and red hair. He had to have an artistic bent to have wound the lengths of his hair around the top of his head to disguise his onsetting baldness. Something attracted me, but what was it? Surely not his academic preparation, although it was far ahead of his time, and light-years ahead of our congregation. He wasn't an athlete and thought the Kansas City Blues (baseball team) was a jazz tune from one of the emporiums on Twelfth Street.

After eight years of listening to his preaching and observing his life, it became obvious that I was impressed to follow his leadership because he was real. During this time of graduating from high school, serving in the Navy, choosing a vocation, selecting a wife, and changing my vocation from marketing to religious education, he taught me some powerful lessons in life. Here are a few of them, couched in their settings.

*1. Love Your Enemies.* World War II was not a popular time to preach this supreme example of love. While the newspapers preached hatred via propaganda, Swadley prayed for the Germans, Italians, and the Japanese as much as for our Allied forces. When his fellow pastors snickered at his "pacifist learnings," he maintained that peace should prevail over war—thirty years ahead of his time.

After hearing his sermon, I was a confused seeker. Even though Jesus said it, I couldn't accept loving enemies into my emotional system. So I went by his house and quizzed him about it. That didn't help much. However, in the next few years, he showed me by his actions. Our church must have had too much of his "far-out Christianity" because it eventually fired him. He reacted by calling the people together to pray for them—sincerely to pray for them.

*2. Love Your Wife.* During our premarital counseling, he shared the depth of his giant heart regarding his boundless love for his wife. He interpreted the love chapter of Corinthians to Opha and me, and then used it as the basis of our wedding vows. Always did he prefer his wife above himself and his children. My parents ably taught the same lesson in the context of our home. Swadley taught it in the context of the Scriptures.

3. *Love Your Church.* Where does a pastor go when fired by the congregation? Some go crazy. Others go into secular work. Swadley went to prayer, and shortly was serving in a desolate place in northwest Missouri. I met him at the Southern Baptist Convention shortly after the trauma and relocation. I was bitter. He was forgiving. In my immaturity I asked him how he could be happy in his new location. His words are seared on my memory. "When you are in God's will, in God's church, with God's people, you will always be happy." He was happy and productive until his recent death.

And you ask, why are these vignettes included in a management book case study? I'll tell you why. To be truthful, he was not the living example of an effective administrator. Then why is he the case study for the final chapter on success? The answer is simple. He achieved his objectives in life, as measured by his value system, as much or more than any other man I have ever known. And my friends, that is success!

# Notes

## CHAPTER 1

1. Lyle E. Schaller and Charles A. Tidwell, *Creative Church Administration* (Nashville: Abingdon, 1975).

2. Katherine Jillson and Preston G. McLean, *The Manager: His Job, His Work and His Self-Respect* (New York: AMA Survey Reports, 1975), p. 1.

## CHAPTER 2

1. Laurence J. Peter and Raymond Hull, *The Petrer Principle: Why Things Always Go Wrong* (New York: Morrow, 1969).

2. George S. Odiorne, *Management by Objective* (New York: Pitman Publishing Corporation, 1965).

CHAPTER 3

1. Robert E. Bingham and Ernest Loessner, *Serving with the Saints* (Nashville: Broadman Press, 1970).

2. Lyle E. Schaller and Charles A. Tidwell, *Creative Church Administration,* p. 55 ff.

3. Raymond O. Loen, *Manage More By Doing Less* (New York: McGraw-Hill Book Company, 1972), p. 194.

4. Leslie E. This, *A Guide to Effective Management* (Reading, Mass.: Addison-Wesley Publishing Co., 1974), pp. 179–180.

5. Schaller and Tidwell, pp. 55–56.


CHAPTER 4

1. B. C. Forbes, comp., *The Forbes Scrapbook of Thoughts on the Business of Life* (New York: Forbes Inc., 1950), p. 121.

2. *Technology Review,* October–November, 1974, p. 8.

3. W. H. Weiss, *Supervision* (Burlington, Iowa: National Research Bureau, Inc., 1973).

4. Raymond O. Loen, *Manage More By Doing Less* (New York: McGraw-Hill Book Company, 1971), pp. 219–220.

5. Charles H. Kepner and B. B. Tregoe, *The Rational Manager* (New York: McGraw-Hill Book Company, 1965), pp. 48–50.


CHAPTER 6

1. *Managers' Forum,* September 1976, p. 2.


CHAPTER 7

1. Carl Bernstein and Bob Woodward, *All the President's Men* (New York: Warner Books, 1975), pp. 294–295.

2. From *The Modern Language Bible, The New Berkeley Version.* Copyright 1945, 1959, © 1969 by Zondervan Publishing House. Used by permission.

3. From *The Four Gospels* translated by E. V. Rieu. Copyright © 1953 by Penguin Press, Ltd.

4. From *The New Testament, a Translation in the Language of the People,* by Charles B. Williams. Copyright 1937 and 1966. Moody Press, Moody Bible Institute of Chicago. Used by permission.

5. *The Forbes Scrapbook,* op. cit., p. 380.

6. Ibid., p. 393.